Faith and Reason

THREE VIEWS

EDITED BY Steve Wilkens

WITH CONTRIBUTIONS BY Craig A. Boyd,
Alan G. Padgett and Carl A. Raschke

IVP Academic

An imprint of InterVarsity Press
Downers Grove, Illinois

InterVarsity Press
P.O. Box 1400, Downers Grove, IL 60515-1426
World Wide Web: www.ivpress.com
Email: email@ivpress.com

InterVarsity Press® is the book-publishing division of InterVarsity Christian Fellowship/USA®, a movement of students and faculty active on campus at hundreds of universities, colleges and schools of nursing in the United States of America, and a member movement of the International Fellowship of Evangelical Students. For information about local and regional activities, write Public Relations Dept., InterVarsity Christian Fellowship/USA, 6400 Schroeder Rd., P.O. Box 7895, Madison, WI 53707-7895, or visit the IVCF website at www.intervarsity.org.

Design: Cindy Kiple
Interior design: Beth Hagenberg
Images: The Incredulity of St. Thomas by Michelangelo Merisi de Caravaggio/Schloss Sanssouci, Potsdam,
        Brandenburg, Germany/The Bridgeman Art Library

ISBN 978-0-8308-4040-3 (print)
ISBN 978-0-8308-8023-2 (digital)

Printed in the United States of America ∞

Library of Congress Cataloging-in-Publication Data
Faith and reason : three views / edited by Steve Wilkens ; with
contributions by Craig Boyd, Alan G. Padgett and Carl Raschke.
     pages cm
  Includes bibliographical references and index.
  ISBN 978-0-8308-4040-3 (pbk. : alk. paper)
1. Faith and reason--Christianity. I. Wilkens, Steve, 1955- II. Boyd,
Craig A. III. Padgett, Alan G., 1955- IV. Raschke, Carl A.
BT50.F346 2014
231'.042--dc23

2014011881

P	21	20	19	18	17	16	15	14	13	12	11	10	9	8	7	6	5	4	3	2	1
Y	32	31	30	29	28	27	26	25	24	23	22	21	20	19	18	17	16	15	14

Contents

Introduction

Steve Wilkens

Life confronts us with an endless stream of questions. Where should I go for lunch? Is it time to buy a new coat? Should I head for bed now or stay up and watch the show I recorded? Paper or plastic? Questions of this variety are rather mundane, and our decisions about them, at least taken separately, have little effect on the overall course of our life. At times, though, we contemplate inquiries that take us to a deeper dimension, a place where our decisions have profound implications. Is there a God? If so, how can I know that, or know anything about who or what God is? What sources and authorities can I trust in my pursuit of truth, or is the quest for truth an elusive dream? How should I live and what should I value? Do I really have any choice in what I value or how I live? Is my life meaningful, or am I simply the accidental result of blind material forces? What happens at the end of my biological existence?

These and similar questions draw us into the most important ponderings of human inquiry. Because they are fundamental, we all ask these questions at some point. Sometimes they arise in crisis situations when events force our attention in their direction; occasionally they come in quiet, reflective moments while sipping coffee in front of a fire or rocking a child to sleep. However, we sometimes work through these deep questions in a more intentional and systematic manner, perhaps in an educational setting or more informally by sustained reading and reflection. When this is the case, we generally refer to this activity as either *theology* or *philosophy*.

Theology and philosophy have never been able to completely distance themselves from each other precisely because they have a shared interest in matters of deep existential concern to us. Yet, although both address the same questions, there are important differences. First, philosophical inquiry is generally understood to be rooted in reason, seeking justification for positions that any clear-thinking person could share. Theology, in contrast, is grounded in revelation, knowledge communicated by God to humanity via Scripture or in some other way. A second difference concerns the proper stance of the individual engaged in these activities. Traditionally, the philosophical ideal is to put aside biases and personal commitments so the best argument can take us where it will. We start, if you will, from a position of detachment and skepticism, evaluating arguments and counterarguments until we arrive at a rational conclusion. Detachment is not an option for faith and theology, however. Theology, as opposed to religious studies,[1] starts from an attitude of trust or faith. In other words, the Christian theologian is committed to beliefs (perhaps as a result of prior philosophical investigations) that are central to the Christian faith.

Because people of faith start from a set of beliefs, certain potential answers to life's big questions will remain viable for a philosopher that will not be options for the Christian. For example, fundamental to Christian faith is a commitment to belief in God's existence. However, philosophers, as philosophers, may remain agnostic or come to a conclusion contrary to that of a Christian. While the philosopher may seriously entertain the belief that human life is accidental or that Scripture is a hindrance in our quest for truth, Christian theology starts from the premise that life is purposeful and the Bible is an authoritative guide to truth. This is not to say that Christians agree on every detail about life's purpose or how we are to understand scriptural authority. Nor, as we will investigate at length in this book, does a believer's commitment allow us

---

[1]The "insider" stance proper to theology is evident in Karl Rahner's definition, which says that "Theology is the conscious and methodical explanation and explication of the divine revelation received and grasped in faith." Quoted from Alister E. McGrath, *Christian Theology: An Introduction* (Malden, MA: Blackwell, 2001), p. 139. By contrast, S. A. Nigosian's view of religious studies stresses the necessity of the "outsider" perspective: "The study of world religions requires an appreciation of the values that each individual religion gives to its believers and an understanding of how people in different times and under different circumstances thought, felt, and acted." S. A. Nigosian, *World Faiths*, 2nd ed. (New York: St. Martin's Press, 1994), p. 15.

to predict how one views faith in relation to philosophy. Instead, the point is that Christianity assumes the truth of basic principles and ideas that philosophers, as philosophers, may view as open questions.

The differences between philosophy and theology concerning authority, stance and method set up the tension this book investigates. Does a shared interest in a common set of questions indicate that philosophy and theology are close kin and allies, or are they competitors vying for our souls, each requiring a loyalty that excludes the other? Do differences in method and orientation signal that these disciplines are valuable and complementary partners, or do their dissimilarities indicate that we should expect philosophy and theology to be incompatible or even mutually hostile?

GETTING BEYOND THE BINARIES

The differences between faith and reason often lead to the assumption that we are confronted by a binary choice—we must choose one or the other. Indeed, individuals on both sides have come close to declaring war on the other. Many who line up on the "reason" side of the line assert that theology and faith are antithetical to clear thought and are inherently hostile to science (which today is often cited as the paramount expression of rational thought). They argue that reliance on faith and the revelation upon which it rests tangles humanity in hopeless and outmoded superstitions that hinder progress. In this view, faith is not benign but dangerous, and thus should be relegated to the dustbins of history.[2] At the other end of the reason-faith spectrum, Christians have often denigrated reason as "merely human," identifying it as the archenemy of faith. In

---

[2]Sigmund Freud declares, "It is not permissible to declare that science is one field of human mental activity and that religion and philosophy are others, at least its equal in value, and that science has no business to interfere with the other two. . . . It is simply a fact that truth cannot be tolerant, that it admits not compromises or limitations, that research regards every sphere of human activity as belonging to it and that it must be relentlessly critical if any other power tries to take over any part of it." Sigmund Freud, "New Introductory Lectures on Psychoanalysis," in *The Complete Introductory Lectures on Psychoanalysis*, ed. and trans. James Strachey (New York: Norton, 1966), p. 624. More recently, Sam Harris says, "For anyone with eyes to see, there can be no doubt that religious faith remains a perpetual source of human conflict. Religion persuades otherwise intelligent men and women to not think, or to think badly, about matters of civilizational importance." Sam Harris, *The End of Faith: Religion, Terror, and the Future of Reason* (New York: Norton, 2005), pp. 236-37.

this view, our very salvation is at stake, so dependence on any finite human capacity threatens or diminishes the faith upon which our eternal destination depends.

While these binary opposites describe perennial and often-popular impressions of the relationship (or lack thereof) between faith and reason, they do not represent the best thinking of either group. Most philosophers today are more circumspect about reason, moderating the Enlightenment's confidence that rationality can transcend the influence of culture, personal bias or perspective, religion, social status and other factors. Indeed, while Christopher Hitchens and others who represent the view that science is the antithesis of faith say, "Our principles are not a faith,"[3] those more careful about the manner in which scientific thought proceeds acknowledge that the scientific enterprise relies on principles that themselves cannot be demonstrated by reason. In addition, science itself relies on the regularities of nature, what we often refer to as the *laws* of nature. However, the laws on which science is grounded are not themselves directly open to empirical confirmation, even if their utility provides good reasons to trust (i.e., have faith in) them. In short, faith of some kind is fundamental to scientific investigation itself.

Similarly, Christians who claim to reject reason's authority inevitably smuggle it back into their considerations in a multitude of ways. They are quite happy to employ the fruits of rational investigation embedded in their cellphone's technology or give thoughtful consideration to retirement investment strategies. Indeed, they may even give reasons, arguments they expect logical individuals to find convincing, for rejecting the spiritual authority of reason. In reality, we all rely on reason in innumerable ways, from balancing the checkbook to reading a map—or reading this page, for that matter. Thus, to make sense of the discussions in this book, we will need to get beyond the stereotypical either/or binaries mentioned above. Instead, the more specific question with which we will struggle concerns the proper relationship of faith and reason, theology and philosophy.

---

[3]Christopher Hitchens, *God Is Not Great: How Religion Ruins Everything* (New York: Twelve, 2009), p. 5.

THE SCOPE OF THE BOOK

Before we move to a general overview of the three positions examined in this book, a few qualifications are in order. First, this book surveys only a subset of the broader topic of the proper relationship between faith and reason. Rather than examining faith as a generic religious concept, our focus is on the relationship between reason and *Christian* faith. Moreover, all three views assume that faith is a necessity for Christian life and that theology is a means of knowing that does not depend on philosophy or any other discipline for its validity. Thus we will not survey variations of the idea that reason equates to, supersedes or renders faith obsolete. In other words, the philosophies of Hegel (who argues that philosophy gives full expression to truths only vaguely discerned by theology), Kant and the deists (who maintain that true religion is that which meets the standard of reason alone), or logical positivism (which places a chasm between truths that can be verified by direct observation and religious claims that can be judged as neither true nor false) will not be examined directly, although all will be addressed tangentially.

Second, each of our views will affirm, in varying ways, the validity of reason and philosophy. This requires that we transcend the caricatured binary oppositions examined above and recognize that the debate is not whether reason has a role for Christians. Instead, our discussion will center on the intellect's proper realm of operation, the necessary conditions for reason's efforts to be of spiritual benefit, and the extent to which reason facilitates an understanding of God, purpose and goodness. Unless we recognize the Christian tradition's affirmation of reason, it is impossible to understand why believers of almost every theological tradition have planted universities wherever they have settled. This is hardly an enterprise for those who reject or denigrate reason.

The third qualification is that, while our contributors each exposit a distinct view of the relationship between faith and philosophy, each of these categories has a number of intramural variations. This should not surprise us, because our three paradigms are relatively broad, and it is not always clear where to place certain thinkers within our categories. In addition, disagreement about the place of philosophy has a history almost as old as Christianity itself. The ancient church contained ardent Christians such as Justin Martyr, Clement, Origen and Augustine who drew on the philosophy of ancient pagans as well as their contemporaries. During this same period, influential leaders such as Tertullian and Tatian were less optimistic about philosophy's use for faith, a sentiment generally echoed by the early monastics and Christian ascetics. A little later on, the medieval church was populated by mystics and contemplatives who sought communion with God by bypassing or transcending reason's powers. However, they shared this historical period with the figures of high scholasticism, who developed rigorous philosophical structures intended to deepen faith and to demonstrate Christianity's truth to the heathen. On this side of the Reformation, the role of the intellect has been emphasized by such diverse groups as Protestant scholasticism and classical Protestant liberalism, while the place of the intellect has been rigorously challenged by groups such as the Pietists, Pentecostals and postmodern Christians. To more clearly understand the contours of the debate about faith and philosophy, we will examine three models—Faith and Philosophy in Tension, Faith Seeking Understanding and the Thomistic Synthesis.

FAITH AND PHILOSOPHY IN TENSION

When Christians and non-Christians alike look for sound bites from prominent believers who appear to support an anti-intellectualist approach, their first stop usually involves one of the representatives of the Faith and Philosophy in Tension (hereafter, Tension position). "Exhibit A" is often provided by one of Christianity's earliest theologians, Tertullian, when he asks, "What indeed has Athens to do with Jerusalem? What concord is there between the Academy and the Church?"[4] These are, of course, rhetorical questions implying that Athens, the cradle of Western philosophy, should be kept separate from Jerusalem, the birthplace of Christian faith. Tertullian appears to have an ally in Martin Luther, who is famous for statements such as: "Reason is the devil's prostitute and can do nothing else but slander and dishonor what God does

---

[4]Tertullian, *On Prescription Against Heretics*, in *The Ante-Nicene Fathers*, vol. 3, ed. Alexander Roberts and James Donaldson (Grand Rapids: Eerdmans, 1951–1957), p. 7.

and says,"[5] and "Reason is the greatest enemy that faith has; it never comes to the aid of spiritual things, but—more frequently than not—struggles against the divine Word, treating with contempt all that emanates from God."[6]

On the surface, these prominent Christians seem to offer a dim assessment of rationality's value. However, there is more to this story than these selective quotes reveal. Tertullian's legal training, which was highly philosophical in orientation, is apparent throughout his work. In fact, his legal/philosophical background supplied language that the church has used for centuries to give expression to trinitarian theology. His writings engaged those he considered heretics in rational arguments, referred to the Stoic philosopher Seneca as "almost one of us,"[7] and claimed that classical philosophers had borrowed many of their ideas from Hebrew Scripture.[8] Similarly, Luther was well versed in philosophy. The nominalist philosophy of his fellow Franciscan William of Occam was a major influence on his insistence on salvation "by faith alone." In the same book where he describes reason as "the greatest enemy that faith has," Luther also argues that, when enlightened by faith, human wisdom is "a fair and glorious instrument, and work of God."[9] At minimum, these factors remind us that dismissing these and other scholars in the Tension camp as anti-intellectual fideists or irrationalists distorts their positions. Instead, understanding how they view faith and philosophy will require a more nuanced perspective, one that holds these two elements in dialectical tension.

I believe it is fair to say that the Tension position encompasses a greater number of variations than the other two we will consider in this book. At the same time, these variations can be placed in two basic categories. First, many who embrace the Tension view emphasize the vast *ontological distance* that distinguishes Creator from creation. God's transcendence, this perspective argues, necessitates that the means by which

[5]Martin Luther, *Luther's Works: Church and Ministry II*, ed. Conrad Bergendoff (Philadelphia: Muhlenberg Press, 1958), 40:175.
[6]Martin Luther, *Table Talk*, trans. William Hazlitt (New York: Dutton, 1960), CCCLIII.
[7]Tertullian, *De anima*, in *The Ante-Nicene Fathers*, 3:20.
[8]Tertullian, *Apology*, in *The Ante-Nicene Fathers*, 3:47.
[9]Luther, *Table Talk*, CCXCIV.

we know of God differ from the process by which we come to other types of knowledge. This does not mean that rational processes have no value. Advocates of this model will affirm that reason is well suited for navigating questions about the created order, such as selecting the best tires for snowy surfaces, providing proper drainage for a parking lot, or setting a broken bone. However, we do not operate only in a world of atoms, flora and human beings. We live also in the presence of the Creator who is Other than creation. Because God inhabits a completely different category of reality, the logic of God differs radically from what we consider rational in the creaturely world. Indeed, because of the ontological distance between God and human beings, God's actions may be viewed as wholly irrational from the human perspective. This dialectic between the knowledge of the created order and knowledge of the divine is often related to a distinction between will and reason. Our task is not to comprehend God's ways through rational means. Instead, salvation requires faith, trust and commitment, which are movements of the will.

A second category within the Tension view places emphasis on the *moral/spiritual distance* that distinguishes God from creation. To be sure, all three views take sin and its effects seriously. However, the Tension view is distinct in its view that sin's lingering effects continue to diminish and distort reason's capacity to comprehend divine truth even after regeneration. Thus reliance upon rationality to discern the nature and ways of God does more harm than good. Stated otherwise, the Tension position is pessimistic about the value of general revelation even after redemption, placing the emphasis on special revelation as the final arbiter of spiritual matters.

As we will see below, some individuals and theological traditions within the Tension category place the emphasis on reason's diminished usefulness because of the ontological distance that separates creature and Creator, while others will stress our moral/spiritual distance from God. However, these themes are not mutually exclusive, and sometimes both appear as complementary features within versions of the Tension model.

One example of placing the emphasis on ontological distance is found within Christian mysticism. Early forms of Christian mysticism were influenced by Neoplatonism, which stresses the ineffable character of the divine.[10] As a result, theological approaches influenced by Neoplatonism often espouse the *via negativa* (or apophatic theology), the view that God is so transcendent that human reason and experience provide no appropriate positive analogies to describe God. Rather than revealing the transcendent God, reason's finite capacities yield only a finite god, resulting in idolatry. Therefore, we can only say what God is not.

Many forms of Christian mysticism argue that the ontological otherness of God requires a unique means of apprehending God. This leads to a contrast between rational forms of knowledge and the moral/spiritual path to rightly conceiving of God. The anonymous medieval work *The Cloud of Unknowing* offers such a contrast. "For of all other creatures and their works, yea, and of the works of God's self, may a man through grace have fullhead of knowing, and well he can think of them: but of God Himself can no man think. . . . By love may He be gotten and holden; but by thought never."[11] With this sort of perspective, we see a clear delineation between two spheres. Reason is a useful tool for earthly matters. However, as the title of *Unknowing* emphasizes, our apprehension of God requires that we "unlearn" pretensions of gaining knowledge by human reason and, instead, strive to know God through love.

The idea of love as a form of knowledge brings us to another motif often present in the Tension position. Dispassionate reason provides understanding of objects. However, love is never detached, and God is subject, not an object. Thus the means by which God is truly apprehended is not the use of detached and objective reason. Instead, God is known via the volitional and personal approach of love and trust. A related idea is found in James K. A. Smith's appraisal of Pentecostal contri-

---

[10]Plotinus, for example, says that, "The One is all things and no one of them; the source of all things is not all things; all things are its possession—running back, so to speak, to it—or, more correctly, not yet so, they will be." Plotinus, *Enneads*, trans. Stephen MacKenna and B. S. Page, 2nd ed. (New York: Pantheon, 1957), 5.2.1.

[11]*The Cloud of Unknowing*, trans. Evelyn Underhill, 2nd ed. (London: John M. Watkins, 1922), p. 6. As an illustration of how the Tension view sometimes finds justification in both the transcendence of God (see quote above) and the effects of sin, Underhill says later in this text, "Reason is a power through the which we depart the evil from the good, the evil from the worse, the good from the better, the worse from the worst, the better from the best. Before ere man sinned, might Reason have done all this by nature. But now it is so blinded with the original sin, that it may not can work this work, unless it be illumined by grace" (ibid., p. 64).

butions to philosophy. He argues that the "openness" of the universe to God and the fact that Christianity requires "affective understanding" mean that Enlightenment notions of knowledge should not dictate the terms of belief.[12] Instead, there are ways of knowing that are heart centered rather than head centered.

Nicolas of Cusa links the themes of "unlearning" and affective understanding with another common element of the Tension position—paradox. He asks us to imagine a circle that contains an inscribed square with each of its corners touching a point on the circle. A mystery becomes evident when we modify the square by increasing the number of sides. As more straight lines are added to what is now an inscribed polygon, its shape paradoxically conforms more closely to that of the circle, which has no straight lines. Yet, "even if the number of its angles is increased *ad infinitum*, the polygon never becomes equal [to the circle] unless it is resolved into an identity with the circle."[13] Recognition that as the number of sides in a polygon increases so also does its conformity to the shape of the circle, which lacks any straight lines, throws us into paradox. This reveals that "the intellect, which is not truth, never comprehends truth so precisely that truth cannot be comprehended infinitely more precisely."[14] It is within the mystery of paradox that we are drawn back to a sense of wonder and awe that opens our will to trust in that which transcends rational comprehension.

A more recent example of paradox in Tension thinking appears in Blaise Pascal's philosophy. His *Pensées* is full of observations of the paradoxes of human existence, but perhaps the defining paradox arises with the question of God's existence. On the one hand, reason provides enough evidence of God's existence that it is irrational to disbelieve. On the other hand, reason is insufficient to provide certainty about God's existence. Thus reason draws us into a paradox: it is neither rational nor irrational to believe in God. This paradox is heightened by the reality that we *cannot not* choose. Of the question

[12]James K. A. Smith, *Thinking in Tongues: Pentecostal Contributions to Christian Philosophy* (Grand Rapids: Eerdmans, 2010), pp. 12-13, 26-27.
[13]*On Learned Ignorance*, trans. Jasper Hopkins, 2nd ed. (Loveland, CO: Arthur J. Banning, 1985), 1.3.10. This paradox is, by the way, the origin of the phrase "squaring the circle."
[14]Ibid.

of God's existence in Pascal's famous "wager," he states: "But you must wager. There is no choice; you are already committed. Which will you choose?"[15]

A similar call to the urgency of choice is found in Søren Kierkegaard's statement that

> Our age is essentially one of understanding and reflection, without passion, momentarily bursting into enthusiasm, and shrewdly relapsing into repose. . . . Nowadays, not even a suicide kills himself in desperation. Before taking the step he deliberates so long and carefully that he literally chokes himself with thought. It is even questionable whether he ought to be called a suicide, since it is really thought which takes his life. He does not die with deliberation but from deliberation.[16]

Both Pascal and Kierkegaard recognize that rational uncertainty may become an excuse to postpone a decision about where we will stand in relationship to God. Cool rationality, after all, demands the time and leisure to work through every angle of a question before making a commitment. However, Thomas Morris tells us that Pascal's *Pensées* was written "to shock his indifferent friends out of their apathy and goad them into a philosophical and religious line of inquiry about life."[17]

The quote above offers a critical insight into the emphasis placed on the urgency of choice by Pascal and Kierkegaard. A purely rational approach to spiritual matters asks only whether an idea is factually true. For the Tension position, this is the wrong question. Even if logic provides an intellectually satisfying conclusion, it leaves unanswered the bigger question of how we are related to God. In short, the rationalist approach, to the extent that it remains in the realm of thought, does not address the question of salvation. Salvation is a matter of faith, and faith questions can only be resolved in the sphere of the will, not in the sphere of reason.

Because the Tension position decisively emphasizes the role of faith

---

[15]Blaise Pascal, *Pensées*, trans. A. J. Krailsheimer (New York: Penguin, 1966), §418.

[16]Søren Kierkegaard, *The Present Age* and *The Difference Between a Genius and an Apostle*, trans. Alexander Dru (New York: Harper & Row, 1962), p. 33.

[17]Thomas V. Morris, *Making Sense of It All: Pascal and the Meaning of Life* (Grand Rapids: Eerdmans, 1992), p. 15.

and choice over reason, Pascal, Kierkegaard and others who hold this position are often considered irrationalists. However, this categorization overlooks some crucial factors. First, reason plays a role in salvation by revealing its own limitations and inadequacies. It confronts us with the paradox of evidence that is simultaneously "enough" and "not enough" for belief in God and thrusts us into the situation in which we must exercise faith.

Second, reason's "negative knowledge," knowledge of its own boundaries, sets the stage for a contrast between the "objective" knowledge of discursive reason and personal knowledge. In this case, personal knowledge takes two forms. First, reason's inability to attain certainty stands as a stark reminder that we are not God. This knowledge is more than just comprehension of a metaphysical fact. At its deepest level, this self-knowledge is an acknowledgment that we are finite and fallen beings who stand before a holy and infinite God. Thus, while reason itself is not faith, this self-knowledge is the condition for becoming open to reliance on the transcendent God. Second, this model challenges the supremacy of detached, impersonal knowledge by positing that personal, subjective knowledge is the means by which we know God. To use Pascal's words, Christianity's call is to know the "God of Abraham, God of Isaac, God of Jacob," not a God who is the logical construct of "the philosophers and scholars."[18] The latter is knowledge *about* God; it views God as an object to be analyzed from a distance. For all its value, objective knowledge cannot bring us into relationship with God. For that, we must *know* God as Abraham, Isaac and Jacob knew God—as a person rather than object. This type of knowing is rooted in personal encounter and trust, not in detached observation and analysis.

Finally, some Christians embrace the Tension paradigm as a result of their understanding of sin's continuing effects. For example, the Formula of Concord says that, although believers

are regenerate and renewed in the spirit of their mind, yet in the present

---

[18]The source of these phrases is "Pascal's Memorial," a scrap of paper on which he recorded an account of a deep religious experience, often referred to as his "night of fire." Pascal sewed this paper into the lining of his coat, where it was discovered upon his death.

life this regeneration and renewal is not complete, but only begun, and
believers are, by the spirit of their mind, in a constant struggle against the
flesh, that is, against the corrupt nature and disposition which cleaves to
us unto death.

The formula goes on to state that "this old Adam . . . still inheres in the
understanding, the will, and all the powers of man."[19] "This old Adam,"
therefore, requires that Christians, even after salvation, remain modest
about the mind's ability to discover or recognize truth.

This view of sin's tenacity contextualizes negative comments concerning reason that appear in Luther, the spiritual father of Concord. For
example, in the passage in which he describes reason as "the devil's
whore," Luther is criticizing those he believes have arrived at their conclusions about baptism by reason alone. In contrast, Luther states that
"we first want to prove our faith, not by setting forth capitals or periods
or *touto tauta* but by clear, sober passages from Scripture which the devil
will not overthrow."[20] Thus the rather indelicate designation of reason as
"the devil's whore" is not a denigration of reason per se, but a condem-
nation of prioritizing rationality over Scripture.

The Formula of Concord's position corresponds to Luther's notion of
the "two kingdoms." One kingdom, the earthly kingdom, is given by God
to govern the earthly affairs of life. In view of human sin, secular powers,
which Luther refers to as God's "left hand," exert their influence by law
and coercion. By this means, God uses the earthly kingdom to provide
order and justice, which are facilitated by our rational capacities.
However, those who administer this power do so only in a very imperfect
manner and from unholy and rebellious motives. God's "right hand" is
a spiritual kingdom revealed in Scripture alone and governed by grace.
Both kingdoms exist side by side in this life, and Christians live in the

---

[19]"The Epitome of the Formula of Concord," in *Concordia: The Lutheran Confessions*, ed. Paul
Timothy McCain, 2nd ed. (St. Louis: Concordia, 2006): 6.4.

[20]Ibid. A similar contrast is seen in another location where Luther refers to reason as a "lovely
whore." He follows this immediately by stating that reason "wants to be wise, and what she says,
she thinks, is the Holy Spirit." Martin Luther, *Luther's Works: Sermons I*, ed. and trans. John W.
Doberstein (Philadelphia: Muhlenberg, 1958), 51:374. Thus Luther is not disparaging reason,
but is instead countering fanaticism and immorality that is justified by reason against what he
sees as the clear witness of special revelation.

ambiguity of citizenship in both worlds. This dual citizenship on the corporate level parallels the individual Christian's dual identity as *simul justus et peccator* ("simultaneously justified and sinner"), described in the Formula of Concord above.

The Anabaptist tradition also adheres to a "two kingdoms" model, but one that differs significantly from Luther's. Instead of dual kingdoms, each ordained by God, Anabaptists view the church as an expression of God's kingdom, while the other kingdom, generally referred to as "the world," stands in opposition to it. "The world" uses material and military power, not as an agent of God's will, but in direct rebellion against God's kingdom and its values. Therefore, the church's call is to separate itself from the world as a witness to the power of love and sacrifice exemplified in the life and death of Christ. As Stanley Hauerwas puts it, "The church first serves the world by helping the world to know what it means to be the world. For without a 'contrast model' the world has no way to know or feel the oddness of its dependence on power for survival."[21] While the Anabaptist "two kingdoms" doctrine starkly differs from the Lutheran paradigm in this regard, it also represents a Tension in that the logic of God's kingdom differs from the fallen and rebellious strategies embedded in earthly reason.

My summary of the Tension paradigm has touched on various expressions ranging from the church fathers up to the nineteenth century. Carl A. Raschke, professor of religious studies at the University of Denver, will extend this discussion beyond the borders of my survey by giving careful attention to biblical support for the Tension view and then drawing ably from contemporary sources to bolster his perspective. In his argument that the message of the gospel represents a radical departure from both Greek and Enlightenment philosophical categories, you will detect echoes of the themes above in his affirmation that the believer's mandate is not intellectual comprehension of an abstract and impersonal God, but trust in the resurrected and risen Christ. A major theme in Raschke's chapter is that whenever Christians have depended on philosophical means to justify or express the Christian faith, the

---

[21]Stanley Hauerwas, *A Community of Character: Toward a Constructive Christian Social Ethic* (Notre Dame: University of Notre Dame Press, 1991), p. 50.

gospel message of personal trust and relationship with the living God has suffered.

FAITH SEEKING UNDERSTANDING

Two recurring themes in the Tension view provide a segue to the Faith Seeking Understanding (hereafter FSU) position. The first is an agreement with Tension thinking about the corrosive effect of sin on both our rational and volitional powers. Both camps believe that, as a result of this corruption, reason cannot aid us in acquiring salvation. The second point of contact is the emphasis placed on the primacy of the will. If faith belongs to the category of volition, questions about salvation find their center in this capacity, not reason.

Perhaps the most important dividing line between Tension and FSU is the role of reason in the life of the Christian. FSU argues that God's salvific work restores both reason and will to the extent that reason can be of spiritual benefit to the believer. However, returning to the second connection cited above between the two views, the will retains a primacy over reason in that the latter is not capable of its most important tasks until the will has been renewed and made capable of desiring to know rightly. Although we could cite numerous advocates of this position, we will focus attention on a line that begins with Augustine, moves to the great medieval intellectual and ecclesial figure Anselm of Canterbury, and finally finds expression in the theology of John Calvin. While the two later figures differ in some details from Augustine's ideas, his influence is evident in their thought.

Prior to his conversion to Christianity, Augustine had a strong affinity for Neoplatonic thought, and even after coming to faith he says that "Those Platonist writings conveyed in every possible way, albeit indirectly, the truth of God and his Word."[22] This "truth of God" Augustine finds in the Platonists can be identified as such because human rationality provides a point of contact with the divine. In short, our nature as thinking beings reflects the rational nature of our Creator. However, Augustine's agreement with Platonism on this point is tempered by a stark dis-

---

[22]Augustine, *The Confessions*, ed. John E. Rotelle, trans. Maria Boulding (Hyde Park, NY: New City, 1997), 8.3.

agreement on another. The Platonists believed that, when properly informed, reason redirects our volition to desire that which is good. Against this belief, Augustine insists that reason never operates in isolation from volition but is always directed and motivated by our desires. To the unregenerate person, this is a deep problem, because our desires are corrupted by the power of sin and are in rebellion against God. In this rebellious state, there are many things that we do not know, not because the intellect cannot know them, but because our will does not *want* to know them.

Although sin infects and weakens the power of reason, the intellect remains capable of performing the functions that we typically attribute to rationality, even in an unregenerate person. It allows such an individual to comprehend a book, design buildings and diagnose mental disorders. What fallen reason cannot do, however, is allow the unredeemed person to use knowledge toward the highest purpose for which the intellect is designed. Reason's primary task is to draw us toward God, the source and goal of rational thought, in an attitude of trust and love. However, apart from grace, our fallen and corrupt will cannot desire this purpose for reason. Instead, unregenerate reason remains trapped in the prideful illusion that its powers allow us to achieve fulfillment on our own terms.

This background allows us to understand Augustine's famous summary of the relationship between faith and reason. In *Tractates on the Gospel of John*, Augustine says, "If you have not understood, I say, believe. For understanding is the recompense of faith. Therefore, seek not to understand so that you may believe, but believe so that you might understand; for 'unless you believe, you will not understand.'"[23] In this quote, "understanding" entails more than the accumulation of cognitive or technical information. "Understanding" refers to the capacity to put this information into the broader framework of God's desire to save us. This cannot occur until faith has restored the believer's desire to see the higher purpose for which reason is designed and rightly order knowledge toward this purpose.

Unlike the Tension position, however, Augustine argues that faithful Christians are called to make full use of their rational and critical fac-

---

[23] Augustine, *Tractates on the Gospel of John: 28-54*, in *The Fathers of the Church*, vol. 3, trans. John W. Rettig (Washington, DC: Catholic University of America Press, 1993), 29.6.

ulties so that they can understand and express what they believe by faith. Indeed, he states that, while rational analysis cannot improve or add to the truths of special revelation, it can correct our interpretations of revelation and aid in understanding how we apply revealed truths to specific situations. At the same time, Augustine maintains that many truths of faith transcend the comprehension of natural reason. Thus, in his discussion of the virgin birth and resurrection of Jesus, he argues that "Faith gives the understanding *access* to these things, unbelief *closes* the door to them."[24] Through faith's eyes, we are able to discern a logic that transcends the power of reason alone.

Although Augustine's approach to faith and philosophy was challenged by scholars in the later medieval period, his theological authority in the centuries immediately following his death was profound. This influence is evident in Anselm, viewed by many as the most important theologian of the early scholastic period. Anselm's most famous piece of philosophical theology has come to be known as the ontological argument for God's existence.[25] In it, Anselm seems to depart from Augustine's FSU approach, because his argument states that our ability to conceive of a perfect being logically leads to the conclusion that such a being (God) actually exists. In short, Anselm seems to say that all people have an innate knowledge of God's existence, and all that is necessary to arrive at this conclusion is careful analysis of the concept of perfection. This appears to be consistent with Anselm's preface to *Cur Deus Homo* ("why God became human"), in which he identifies two goals: answering the "objections of unbelievers who reject the Christian faith because they think it contrary to reason" and "setting Christ aside (as if he had never been) prov[ing] by logical arguments that it is impossible for any man to be saved without Him."[26] These elements lead many to believe that Anselm has a higher degree of confidence than Augustine

---

[24] Augustine, *"The Confessions" and The Letters of St. Augustin*, in *A Select Library of the Nicene and Post-Nicene Fathers*, vol. 1, series 1, ed. Phillip Schaff (Grand Rapids: Eerdmans, 1956), *Ep.* 137.15.

[25] For this argument, see Anselm, *Complete Philosophical and Theological Treatises of Anselm of Canterbury*, trans. Jasper Hopkins and Herbert Richardson (Minneapolis: Arthur J. Banning, 2000), *Proslogion* 1–5.

[26] Anselm, *Cur Deus Homo* (London: Griffith, Farran, Okeden and Welsh, 1890), preface.

that unaided human reason can grasp theological truths.

However, Anselm's work also includes aspects that bring his view of faith and reason into close connection with Augustine's position. For one thing, *Proslogion*, the book in which Anselm's argument appears, is written as a prayer, an odd genre if one intends to prove God's existence by reason alone. Moreover, it is hard to overlook Anselm's homage to Augustine in the original title for this brief text—"Faith Seeking Understanding"—and we see this reinforced in the statement that appears immediately prior to his argument for God's existence: "For I do not seek to understand in order to believe, but I believe in order to understand. For I believe even this: that unless I believe, I shall not understand."[27] Further, in this same context Anselm identifies human sinfulness and the resulting distortion of desire as the obstacle preventing reason from seeing clearly the truths of God that lead to human happiness.[28]

In short, Anselm's thought shows strong Augustinian affinities in his belief that we cannot fully grasp the ultimate purpose of theological truths apart from the restoration of our will. Nonetheless, even if we do not read Anselm's philosophical theology as rational proofs aimed at convincing the skeptic, it is clear that he is convinced that reason cannot contradict revelation. Thus he actively advocates the application of philosophical categories to theological matters by Christians. However, looking again at the material at the beginning of our examination of Anselm, it appears that he goes somewhat beyond Augustine by arguing that philosophy can demonstrate to the unbeliever that Christianity's doctrines are not irrational (a goal more modest than proof). However, Anselm retains a level of intellectual restraint by reminding readers that while redeemed reason can demonstrate *that* Christianity's claims are rational, it is limited in fully explaining *how* they are true.[29]

---

[27]Anselm, *Proslogion* 1.

[28]"O the unhappy fate of man when he lost that [end] for which he was made! O that hard and ominous fall! Alas, what he lost and what he found, what vanished and what remained! He lost the happiness for which he was made and found an unhappiness for which he was not made" (ibid.).

[29]In *Monologium*, Anselm says that "When investigating the inexplicable, if it is possible to arrive at an account which is certainly correct, I think one must be content with that even if it is impossible to see how it may be so." Anselm, *Monologium*, in *The Major Works of Anselm of Canterbury* (Charlottesville, VA: InteLex, 2006), p. 64.

Like so many other Christian scholars, John Calvin can sound either like a committed rationalist or an unrepentant irrationalist when selectively read. Thus, on the one hand, he asks,

> Shall we say that the philosophers were blind in their fine observations and artful description of nature? Shall we say that those men were devoid of understanding who conceived the art of disputation and taught us to speak reasonably? Shall we say that they are insane who developed medicine, devoting their labor to our benefit? What shall we say of all the mathematical sciences? Shall we consider them the ravings of madmen? No, we cannot read the writings of the ancients on these subjects without great admiration. We marvel at them because we are compelled to recognize how preeminent they are.[30]

On the other hand, commenting on 1 Corinthians 1:20, Calvin writes that "man with all his shrewdness is as stupid about understanding by himself the mysteries of God as an ass is incapable of understanding musical harmony."[31]

While the quotes above may seem contradictory, they come together when we recognize that Calvin's primary concern is soteriological rather than epistemological. In other words, the highest expressions of the art of disputation, medicine and the mathematical sciences, as valuable as they may be, cannot lead us to salvation, or what Augustine and Anselm might have called "understanding." The failure of these intellectual pursuits to point us toward God is not due to a lack of revelation. Nor is God to be blamed for creating humans with intellectual powers deficient in their ability to discern the available revelation. Indeed, reason's power would have been sufficient to rightly discern God's revelation through creation (even if not completely) "if Adam had remained upright."[32]

Even in our fallen state, Calvin says, "There is within the human mind, and indeed by natural instinct, an awareness of divinity."[33] This awareness of God, the *sensus divinitatas*, is a sign of God's invitation to faith.

---

[30]John Calvin, *Institutes of the Christian Religion*, 2 vols., ed. John T. McNeill, trans. Ford Lewis Battles (Philadelphia: Westminster Press, 1960), 2.2.15.

[31]John Calvin, *Calvin's New Testament Commentaries: 1 Corinthians*, ed. David W. Torrance and Thomas F. Torrance, trans. John W. Fraser (Grand Rapids: Eerdmans, 1996), p. 38.

[32]Calvin, *Institutes* 1.2.1.

[33]Calvin, *Institutes* 1.3.1.

However, this gift of grace is a double-edged sword, since humans, under sin's influence, fail to use this knowledge as God intends. Thus Calvin says, "they are condemned by their own testimony because they have failed to honor him and to consecrate their lives to his will."[34]

The story is different for those whose will has been restored so that reason is now subject to the Holy Spirit and thus properly oriented toward God. It is part of the Christian's duty to employ intellectual faculties in service of faith. Reason is, after all, God's gracious gift, and when rightly subjugated to divine authority, it assists us in comprehending and applying Scripture's truth to the diverse dimensions of human existence. However, Calvin remains constantly vigilant about the danger of autonomous reason and emphasizes the instrumental use of reason. We are to ground ourselves first in what is clearly known by means of Scripture. Only then does reason come into play as a means of analyzing and organizing that which God reveals.

Our advocate for the FSU position is Alan G. Padgett, professor of systematic theology at Luther Seminary. Dr. Padgett will echo FSU's rejection of the notion that our rational processes are value-neutral, objective and exempt from sin's effects. Thus he argues that faith is necessary to reorient our rational capacities to the purposes for which God intends them. At the same time, Padgett encourages a mutuality model in which philosophy critiques our theology, explores the ramifications of our belief and its connections to every aspect of life, and deepens our understanding of and gratitude toward God.

THE THOMISTIC SYNTHESIS

The difference between FSU and the Thomistic Synthesis (hereafter TS) is often a matter of degree. Both views agree that truths about God are accessible to reason but that such truths are hazy, partial and insufficient for salvation. Thus each says that redemption, like a set of corrective lenses, brings into focus what was only vaguely discerned by reason through general revelation. The main dividing point between these positions is whether truths derived by philosophical means can aid us in

---

[34]Calvin, *Institutes* 1.3.1.

acquiring salvation. FSU maintains that unregenerate reason only drives us deeper into sin. In contrast, the TS argues that the degree of truth and beauty available to reason's natural powers is like a signpost that can point us in the direction of salvation and the deeper spiritual truths available through special revelation. In other words, there is a synthesis of philosophy and theology in which natural reason acts as a "hand-maiden" to theology by preparing people to receive salvation.

Since our third view of faith and reason has been labeled the Thomistic Synthesis, it might seem anachronistic to seek exemplars for this position prior the work of its namesake, Thomas Aquinas, in the thirteenth century. This is true to the extent that Aquinas offers a system that, as a whole, is innovative. However, his synthesis incorporates ideas about reason's access to divine realities held in previous centuries by Christians and non-Christians alike. More specifically, Aquinas's synthesis draws upon a longstanding affirmation of natural theology, the view that human reason and experience can lead us toward reliable (which is not to say exhaustive) conclusions about God.

Natural theology was widespread in the classical philosophical thought of Plato, Aristotle and the Stoics, to mention just a few exemplars. Confidence in such an approach was grounded in the recognition that philosophical thought led to ideas about realities that had very different characteristics from the material objects of sense experience. For example, my eyes detect physical objects with shapes that we identify as triangular. However, my mind can also conceive of triangularity, a metaphysical concept that transcends the imperfections, corruptibility, transience and particularity that are characteristic of all tangible examples of a triangle. In other words, the "triangularity" my mind grasps has perfections (e.g., eternality, immutability, independence and universality) that are not possessed by any physical triangle that I could create. This leads many to the conclusions that (1) divine reality or realities exist and possess certain perfections, and (2) reason, the power that conceives of these metaphysical realities and qualities, must be the human capacity that corresponds most closely to the divine.

Natural theology is not limited to the classical period. Philosophers throughout history, including many Christians, have concluded that reason's intuitions about the transcendent and divine are necessary to make sense of the observable world. Thus, while Tertullian was dubious of philosophy's assistance in spiritual matters, Clement of Alexandria, who lived around the same time, comes to a different conclusion. He says, "Before the advent of the Lord, philosophy was necessary to the Greeks for righteousness. And now it becomes conducive to piety; being a kind of preparatory training to those who attain to faith through demonstration."[35] Instead of viewing philosophy as contrary to grace, Clement argues that reason's ability to draw people in a Godward direction is a sign of divine grace toward all people, "For God is the cause of all good things."[36] Justin Martyr, who lived in the second century, goes so far as to argue that classical Greek philosophers such as Socrates and Heraclitus who "lived reasonably" are to be considered Christians, even though they lived prior to Christ.[37] Likewise, he argues that Socrates's philosophy points to Christ, "for He [Christ] was and is the Word who is in every man"[38] who lives according to true reason.

Christian thinkers have often pointed to Scripture as a support for their belief that reason directs us toward God. For example, Scripture contains frequent admonitions to pursue wisdom, which is portrayed as a gift from God (1 Kings 3:12; 5:12; Ps 119:98; Prov 2:6) to be coveted as a means to know God's ways (Prov 2:1-5). John's Gospel opens with references to Jesus as the *Logos*, a Greek term widely used by early philosophers to speak of the divine, rational, organizing principle of the universe. Thus John, writing for an audience familiar with these connotations, identifies Jesus as the Divine One in whom all things find their logic.

Perhaps the passage most frequently cited by Christians to bolster arguments for natural theology is Romans 1:20: "For since the creation of the world God's invisible qualities—his eternal power and divine nature—have been clearly seen, being understood from what has been

---

[35]Clement of Alexandria, *Stromata*, in *The Ante-Nicene Fathers*, vol. 2, 1.5. Clement clarifies later that when he speak of philosophy as preparatory training for faith, he is not referring to any particular philosophical school or teacher. Instead, "whatever has been well said by each of those sects, which teach righteousness along with a science pervaded by piety,—this eclectic whole I call philosophy" (1.7).

[36]Clement of Alexandria, *Stromata* 1.5.

[37]Justin Martyr, *Apology*, in *The Ante-Nicene Fathers*, vol. 1, 1.46.

[38]Ibid., 2.10.

made, so that people are without excuse" (NIV). Aquinas appeals to this verse, not just as confirmation of reason's ability to discern God's existence, but also as an indicator of the way natural theology works. Reason does not have access to divine realities directly. Instead, we discern truths about the Creator indirectly through our observation of creation.

Aquinas's epistemological approach signals an important shift. Prior to Aquinas, most Christians employed a Platonic, a priori view of knowledge. One must first know general concepts before being able to recognize the proper place of particular objects that mirror these concepts. This sheds light on why the FSU position sharply distinguishes between reason's ability to acquire information and its ability to acquire what Augustine calls "understanding." Knowledge of the particular and temporary obscures our understanding of the things of God, while an understanding of the perfect and eternal sanctifies our knowledge of the particular and temporary. However, Aquinas is at the vanguard of a Christian rediscovery of Aristotle, a thinker Aquinas admires so much that he simply refers to him as "The Philosopher."[39] Aristotelian philosophy relies on an a posteriori approach, arguing that we move from observation of sensible objects to knowledge of the transcendent truths. This allows Aquinas to embrace the continuity of knowledge, in which knowledge gleaned from the observable realm does not obscure the divine but reveals it.

Because the physical, created order is the effect of a divine cause, philosophy can discern certain truths about God. The "Five Ways," Aquinas's philosophical arguments for God's existence,[40] provide his most famous example of how reason moves from the existence and order of the physical world to the conclusion that it must have a Creator and Designer. Likewise, Aquinas argues that philosophy allows us to discover God's moral expectations for us.[41] Thus he says, "The existence of God and other like truths about God, which can be known by natural reason, are not articles of faith, but are preambles to the articles; for faith presupposes natural knowledge, even as grace presupposes nature, and per-

---

[39]For example, see Thomas Aquinas, *Summa Theologiae* 1.84.a.7.
[40]Ibid., 1.2.a.3.
[41]Ibid., 1-2.94.

fection supposes something that can be perfected."[42]

This quote provides an important key to understanding the TS. While Aquinas believes it is possible to arrive at truths about God apart from faith, these philosophical conclusions alone do not bring us to the ultimate goal toward which reason points. Because these truths are "preambles," one can intellectually affirm God's existence and comprehend one's moral obligations but remain outside the realm of salvation. Only faith prompted by the truths revealed in Scripture brings us to our God-intended telos. Thus philosophy should not be viewed as independent from philosophy, but as an aid that, if used rightly, brings us to the threshold of faith. On the other side of this synthesis, however, theology is independent of philosophy in that "there is nothing to prevent a man, who cannot grasp a proof, accepting, as a matter of faith, something which in itself is capable of being scientifically known and demonstrated."[43]

Because both philosophical truths and theological truths originate in God, Aquinas argues that they cannot come into contradiction. However, there is an advantage to those who come to know truths within the range of reason's abilities through Scripture instead. Apart from divine revelation, "the truth about God such as reason could discover, would only be known by a few, and that after a long time, and with the admixture of many errors." Because our salvation depends on clearly knowing these fundamental truths, "It was therefore necessary that besides philosophical science built up by reason, there should be a sacred science [theology] learned through revelation.[44]

The paragraph above affirms the priority of theology over philosophy in the TS. However, Aquinas views philosophy as an important adjunct (or "handmaiden") to theology for at least three reasons. First, it allows us to see that theological truths do not contradict the truths of reason. Moreover, it has apologetic value. Because philosophy provides reasonable demonstrations of God's existence and attributes, it opens the nonbeliever to the possibility that Christian truths that transcend the power of reason might also be true. Finally, while revelation is infallible, our theology is not. Phi-

[42]Ibid., 1.2.a.2.
[43]Ibid., 1.2.a.2.
[44]Ibid., 1.1.a.1.

losophy helps Christians identify and correct theological mistakes and provides for a systematic expression of our beliefs.

There were large pockets of resistance against the TS view within the Catholic Church immediately after Aquinas's death, but it is widespread within Catholic thought today. For example, the preamble of Pope John Paul II's encyclical *Fides et Ratio* begins, "Faith and reason seem to be like two wings by which the human spirit is raised up toward the contemplation of truth."[45] Perhaps the best-known Thomist of recent years, Etienne Gilson, says, "Faith and Reason can neither contradict each other, nor ignore each other, nor be confused. Reason may well try to justify Faith: it will never transform Faith into Reason, for as soon as Faith were to abandon authority for proof, it would cease to believe; it would know."[46]

While variations of Thomism are generally associated with Catholic scholarship, natural theology has also found advocates among Protestant thinkers. Perhaps the best known is William Paley, who crafted the so-called watchmaker argument for God's existence.[47] This argument, a variation of Aquinas's design argument, states that a person who observes the intricacies of a mechanical watch's inner workings will logically conclude "that the watch must have had a maker; that there must have existed at some time and at some place or other, an artificer or artificers who formed it for the purpose which we find it actually to answer; who comprehended it and designed its use."[48] When one finds intelligence displayed in the interactions of complex systems in which the component parts themselves lack reason, whether a watch or a physical universe, it seems logical to conclude the intelligence of their operations originates in an external, rational being (i.e., God). While Paley argues

---

[45]See Laurence Paul Hemming and Susan Frank Parsons, eds., *Restoring Faith in Reason: With a New Translation of the Encyclical Letter* Faith and Reason *of Pope John Paul II* (Notre Dame: University of Notre Dame Press, 2003), p. 3.

[46]Etienne Gilson, *The Philosophy of St. Thomas Aquinas*, trans. Edward Bullough, 2nd ed. (St. Louis: B. Herder, 1940), p. 52.

[47]Athough the phrase "watchmaker God" often carries negative connotations today, in Paley's time watchmaking was an arduous and highly specialized craft, and so this phrase was used to speak favorably of God's capacity and goodness in the design of a complex and interconnected creation.

[48]William Paley, *Natural Theology*, ed. Matthew D. Eddy and David Knight (New York: Oxford University Press, 2006), p. 8.

that philosophy can arrive at accurate conclusions about the existence and attributes of God, he also insists, like Aquinas, that natural theology must be complemented by revealed religion for us to most fully understand Christianity's truths.

Theologians like Aquinas and Paley maintain that faith stands in continuity with reason but also assign theology an independent and superior role. However, some later advocates of natural theology challenged Aquinas's synthesis. John Locke, for example, does not dispute Aquinas's contention that some truths transcend reason's capacity and can only be known by revelation. Yet Locke holds that the validity of revealed truths is ultimately subject to reason's judgment. While reason cannot directly verify or falsify faith claims, "It still belongs to reason to judge of the truth of its being a revelation. . . . Indeed, if anything shall be thought revelation which is contrary to the plain principles of reason, and the evident knowledge the mind has of its own clear and distinct ideas; there reason must be hearkened to, as to a matter within its province."[49]

Locke's subtle movement toward assigning reason the role of arbiter in determining the validity of revelation is accentuated in deism, which rejects the idea that any claim can be called truth apart from reason's determinations. Deist Matthew Tindal finds the idea of revelation that transcends rational truth offensive to the efficacy of God. "If God has given mankind a law, he must have given them likewise sufficient means of knowing it; he would, otherwise, have defeated his own intent in giving it."[50] Similarly, he argues that the goodness of God requires that all true religion be accessible to all people. Reason, God's gift to humanity, has made the fullness of God's will available to all since creation. Thus the intellect is the final judge of what should be embraced as true reason, and all claims to special revelation that do not conform to reason should be jettisoned as superstition.

Deism's rejection of a special revelation is also a rejection of Aquinas's synthesis, and the reduction of theology to purely rational truth resulted in a significant move away from all forms of natural theology for several

---

[49]John Locke, *An Essay Concerning Human Understanding*, 2 vols. (New York: Dover, 1959), 4.18.8.
[50]Matthew Tindal, *Christianity as Old as the Creation* (Chestnut Hill, MA: Adamant, 2005), 1:5.

centuries, especially in Protestant circles. However, the TS has experienced a resurgence in recent decades and finds an advocate in Craig A. Boyd, associate professor of philosophy at Saint Louis University. Boyd maintains that God creates humans with a purpose and that all the gifts God equips us with, reason included, contribute toward our pursuit of that purpose when properly used. However, the natural gift of reason is completed by the supernatural gift of grace, which provides all that is necessary for our salvation. Thus he gives contemporary expression to Aquinas's conviction that, while we should never view the roles of philosophy and theology as identical, there is a continuity and complementarity that allows grace to bring nature to perfection.

WHORE, HANDMAIDEN OR SOMETHING IN BETWEEN?

There is a potential pitfall in the way we write about faith and philosophy in this book. When detailed arguments are laid out, replete with citations from and references to the Western intellectual tradition's giants, we are tempted to conclude that this is a purely academic exercise. This is indeed an academic exercise, but it is not just that. This exploration starts from a topic that all people, Christian and non-Christian alike, have beliefs about. Every person has ideas about what faith and reason are and what they should or should not do. And we have notions about how faith and philosophy fit together or, perhaps, about how they fail to mesh at all. In other words, because these are beliefs that all people have, they are not just academic questions; they are human questions, and questions that take us into important areas.

While we all have beliefs about the faith/reason connection, it is not necessarily the case that we have come to these beliefs through a careful and informed investigation. In fact, most of us arrive at our views on this topic through absorption rather than adoption. Some have absorbed the view that philosophy is like a whore, seducing us from a true love of God by making false promises. Others have been surrounded by those who see philosophy as the handmaiden to theology, faithfully serving her mistress. Regardless of whether we hold one of these two views or something in between, it may be that we have jumped to our conclusions about the nature of faith and reason and their proper interaction before we have encountered all the options and reflected upon the alternatives.

While certain questions do not require extended examination, I do not think the relationship of philosophy and faith is one of those, especially for Christians. First, this discussion focuses on two capacities that are essential to our humanity: intellect and will. Second, how we understand the proper roles of faith and reason exerts influence on a long list of other important questions. How we understand divine grace is closely connected with our views about faith and reason. Differences about whether Christians should engage in apologetics and what form apologetics should take are correlated with how we think of reason's role in the Christian's life. The degree to which we should expect Christian ethics to agree with or depart from non-Christian moral theories is linked to how we define faith in relationship to philosophy. All Christians agree that sin corrupts, but the extent of this corruption, both before and after redemption, cannot be divorced from how we understand the place of will and reason in salvation and sanctification. In short, our overall theological orientation is shaped by our foundational beliefs about the roles of reason and faith.

Because the topic of this book takes us into areas that are fundamental to our identity as thinkers and believers, it is useful not just to consider these issues carefully but to do so in the company of others who have already engaged this discussion thoughtfully. The three scholars who have contributed their expositions and critiques will offer reasons why their approach provides the best perspective of faith in relation to philosophy. In that process, they will introduce you to others who have helped them contemplate these vital questions and their implications. My hope is that you will allow them to help you navigate, with rigor and joy, one of the most significant discussions of the Christian community.

1

Faith and Philosophy in Tension

Carl A. Raschke

THE GREEK-JEW QUESTION

CHRISTIAN FAITH AND PHILOSOPHY for the most part have been in tension for most of the last two thousand years. Ever since early Christianity spread beyond Roman Judea during the first century, the tension between faith and philosophy has remained largely unresolved. But in order to contextualize this tension, we must first understand some of the major historical factors that gave rise to it in the first place. Faith and philosophy do not exist in a vacuum. While we are often in the habit nowadays of viewing this longstanding and familiar tension as something that has always had the same meaning and importance, both the language of the debates and the controversies have changed radically over the years. For example, until the eighteenth century the challenge to faith from "philosophy" came for the most part from the pagan Greek tradition. From the modern era onward, it emanated from the natural sciences and the efforts of philosophers to adopt the standards of truth-testing to which they believed scientists themselves adhered. In the late nineteenth and twentieth centuries a new challenge came from the social and linguistic sciences, particularly anthropology, which fostered the assumption, often shared by philosophers, that expressions of faith are culturally, morally and conceptually relevant only to their own times. How did these tensions arise? How did they evolve?

If we are to understand the tension more fully, both historically and in the contemporary setting, we must fully recognize, as every student of civilization has learned in textbooks for a century, that virtually every form of what we might broadly call the "Western perspective" reflects this stress. The tension ultimately is derived from the confluence of two ancient cognitive and intellectual watercourses, what we call the Hebraic and the Greco-Roman. This confluence dates back to the fourth century B.C., more than three hundred years before the time of Jesus. It was the direct consequence of the conquest of the Middle East by the armies of Alexander the Great. In order to hold their vast new empire together, Alexander's immediate successors embarked on a campaign of forced cultural assimilation of their new subject peoples. The policy, which required that Greek be spoken everywhere as the official language of diplomacy, commerce, and education and that religious practice conform as much as possible to certain general norms, was known as "Hellenization."

Ancient Judaism, generally left alone by previous conquerors, was pressured into submission as well. While the Jews of this period tended either to accommodate or remain indifferent to Hellenization in the cultural and educational spheres, they fiercely resisted it when it came to standards of worship. The reason was obvious. Greek religion was centered on the veneration and elaboration of visible images of God, or the gods. In contrast, the First Commandment of the Decalogue given by God to Moses on Mount Sinai absolutely prohibited having representations, or "images," of the deity. "You shall have no other gods before me" (Ex 20:3).[1] What the Greeks and other peoples of the Mediterranean considered piety, the Jews regarded as idolatry. The Maccabean Revolt of 167 B.C. was a successful military and political movement in ancient Judea to stem the tide of Hellenization.

Foreign domination of Judea lasted up until the early twentieth century. A century after the Maccabeans overthrew their Hellenic overlords, the Romans marched in and established an even more brutal regime. Unlike the Greeks, however, Roman policy was not designed to suppress or alter Judaic practices, only to prevent political sedition and rebellion. Nevertheless, in A.D. 66 the Jews revolted once more, mainly for political and economic reasons, and were ruthlessly suppressed. A second revolt decades later led to the virtual extermination of Jewish

---

[1]All Scripture quotations, unless otherwise noted, are taken from the NIV.

habitation in Palestine, and the fledgling early Christian movement quickly lost most of its Hebraic characteristics. The wide majority of Christians in the first century identified themselves as Jews, who distinguished themselves from their counterparts mainly by recognizing Jesus of Nazareth as the long-expected Messiah, much like Messianic Judaism today. The upshot of these developments was that Christianity itself became increasingly Hellenized, while the framework for the interpretation of predominantly Hebraic Scripture became the accepted schools of Greek philosophy, specifically Platonism. This process started during the second century with the writings of the so-called Apologists, who sought to convince the Roman authorities of their day that Christianity was not some weird, Asian personality cult, but a respectable type of practical philosophy that conformed to Roman sensibilities and values.

Such historical considerations mainly serve to provide a setting for the debate. Ways of resolving the issue have varied immensely, and the answer seems no clearer today than it did two thousand years ago. The famous question of the late twentieth-century postmodern French philosopher Jacques Derrida—"Are we Jews? Are we Greeks"[2]—echoes the famous comment of the late second-century theologian Tertullian: "What indeed has Athens to do with Jerusalem?"[3] Tertullian's remark, and to a lesser extent Derrida's, are often cited to buttress the view that philosophy should play no role in the defense of faith. But the context of the remark in Tertullian's treatise *On the Prescription of Heretics* shows that Tertullian was mainly arguing against the use of philosophy as a *substitute* for faith, a common strategy of the schismatics of his own day.

The sentence after Derrida's statement underscores the same point. "Are we . . . *first* Jews or *first* Greeks?"[4] Contrary to the conventional wisdom, Tertullian did not reject philosophical approaches per se. He himself was not only a highly educated Roman but also one steeped in the Platonism, Stoicism and Epicureanism of his own age. The work in which his comment appears was aimed specifically at the influential writings

---

[2]Jacques Derrida, *Writing and Difference*, trans. Alan Bass (Chicago: University of Chicago Press, 1978), p. 153.

[3]Tertullian, *De Praescriptione Hereticorum* 7.9, in *The Ante-Nicene Fathers*, vol. 3, ed. Alexander Roberts and James Donaldson (New York: Charles Scribner's Sons, 1903).

[4]Derrida, *Writing and Difference*, p. 153.

of the Gnostics, especially the second-century teacher and church leader Valentinus. According to his critics, Valentinus had urged his adherents, both subtly and not so subtly, to regard the Platonic teachings of his time as superior to the simple testament given in the Gospels and to despise the unlettered and simple-hearted, whom Jesus, for instance, had commended in the Sermon on the Mount. Furthermore, Valentinus had supposedly sought to convince people that the method of *dialectical disputation*—the trotting out of contrary forms of reasoning and articulated positions with the intent of exposing the logical inconsistencies in each that was first employed by Socrates and common among all schools of Greek philosophy—was superior to belief in the saving power of the risen Christ. In other words, Tertullian was not reviling philosophy so much as its *misapplication* in the hands of the learned who had lost all sense of what it means to be a Christ-follower first and an intellectual second. Tertullian was merely embroidering on the sentiment espoused broadly by the apostle Paul in his first letter to the Corinthians: "And so it was with me, brothers and sisters. When I came to you, I did not come with eloquence or human wisdom as I proclaimed to you the testimony about God. For I resolved to know nothing while I was with you except Jesus Christ and him crucified" (1 Cor 2:1-2).

PAUL'S CRITIQUE OF PHILOSOPHY

Paul's sustained argument in 1 Corinthians serves as a paradigm of what for our purposes may be considered the standard example of *faith against philosophy*, or what should preferably be construed as *faith and philosophy in dialectical tension* with each other. Because we call ourselves Christian thinkers with a core conviction that our ultimate authority rests on Scripture, we must take Paul very seriously. Most studies and commentaries on 1 Corinthians stress that Paul is confronting with strong rhetoric of his own, frequently citing or deploying the actual slogans of factions in the church at Corinth, the tendency to confuse submission to Christ with Hellenistic "wisdom" (*sophia*). In the Jewish context of Paul's day "wisdom" meant a kind of special knowledge associated with the study of Torah and, for Gentiles, the sort of esoteric understanding reserved primarily for philosophers. Paul was convinced this misidentification of faith with Hellenistic wisdom fomented a certain arrogance and elitism, distorting the very self-effacement and humility that Jesus had demonstrated in going to the cross that marked the central way of salvation for Christians. Most commentaries on 1 Corinthians tend to emphasize the essential tension between faith and philosophy as comparable to the familiar dialectic between an esoteric knowledge that "puffs up," as Paul puts it in chapter 13, and the *agapē* love shown by the simple-hearted person. It is love that "builds up" the Christian community. Thus Paul's appeal to faith over philosophy is connected essentially with preserving peace within the church.[5]

At the same time, a close reading of Paul's own extended discussion reveals that more is actually at stake. At the outset Paul makes clear that the issue is not primarily an ethical one. It is about the very character of Christian salvation, which turns out to be as much "historical" as personal. "We do, however, speak a message of wisdom among the mature," Paul writes, "but not the wisdom of this age or of the rulers of this age, who are coming to nothing. No, we declare God's wisdom, a mystery that has been hidden and that God destined for our glory before time began. None of the rulers of this age understood it, for if they had, they would not have crucified the Lord of glory" (1 Cor 2:6-8). In other words, the achievement of personal "wisdom" as the means of salvation is from God's perspective completely misguided and useless. The crucifixion is an event that is a once-and-for-all game changer in the story of salvation.

> For since in the wisdom of God the world through its wisdom did not know him, God was pleased through the foolishness of what was preached to save those who believe. Jews demand signs and Greeks look for wisdom, but we preach Christ crucified: a stumbling block to Jews and foolishness to Gentiles, but to those whom God has called, both Jews and Greeks, Christ the power of God and the wisdom of God. (1 Cor 1:21-24)

Just as in Romans Paul challenges the conventional Pharisaic narrative of what it means to be faithful in matters of righteousness before God, so in 1 Corinthians he calls to account the alternative Hellenistic

---

[5]For example, see Anthony C. Thiselton, *The First Epistle to the Corinthians: A Commentary on the Greek Text* (Grand Rapids: Eerdmans, 2000), p. 145.

version that puts such a premium on "theoretical," or philosophical, so-phistication when it comes to working out one's destiny. But Paul is not offering in this situation a "third way" of personal salvation, a new and improved edition of standard spiritual self-help manuals for either Jews or Gentiles. On the contrary, he is presenting a radically new framework for grasping God's general plan for his own chosen people, "those whom God has called" (1 Cor 1:24). The bone of contention here has very little to do with spiritual formation and almost everything to do with how God is using Gentiles, as well as Jews, to accomplish his ultimate purpose for all things.

A clue to this new framework can be found in Paul's employment of the term *skandalon*, or "stumbling block." The term is common in the Septuagint, the Hellenistic translation of the Old Testament into Greek, as well as in the Gospels and in other New Testament literature. As William Barclay points out, the word generally has two sets of connota-tions. It can mean either an obstacle to trip someone up in their forward journey, or it can imply a lure or trap designed to entice someone to destruction.[6] The first meaning is obviously what Paul intended in this instance. Crucifixion was a horrible form of torture devised by the Romans to convey to all onlookers the might of Roman rule by totally obliterating the dignity and identity of anyone who might dare oppose it. Conventional messianic expectations focused on a Jewish emanci-pator who was mightier than the Romans themselves. Hence, the cruci-fixion becomes a stumbling block to the extent that it would be readily and even indignantly dismissed by those whose concept of collective salvation for those who are "called" conforms to the commonsensical or conventional notion.

Acknowledging a crucified messiah as the one true messiah whose "power" is greater than any military general or political genius requires a complete inversion of our understanding of what terms generally signify. It amounts, as the Danish philosopher Søren Kierkegaard would put it 1,900 years later, to taking a "leap" of faith. Traditional messianic antici-pations of "he who is to come" centered on waiting for certain familiar

---

[6]William Barclay, *New Testament Words* (Philadelphia: Westminster Press, 1974), p. 262.

historical "signs" indicating a vaguely defined, yet intuitively cognizable moment of salvation in which those who were wont to regard themselves as chosen could easily recognize. The death of the messiah on the cross was clearly *counterintuitive*. Yet this absurd event, according to Paul, represented the "power of God and the wisdom of God" (1 Cor 1:24). The event cannot be apprehended "rationally," if by such a common philosophical word we mean a sort of proportionality (*ratio*) among the possible semantic extensions that are acceptable within the grammar of the term "messiah." Yet it is a kind of counterwisdom that does not exceed, but *defies*, all such "rationality," and in the process lays the groundwork for what we may consider an "alternative rationality" within the Western philosophical tradition, more congenial to Christian faith, that will emerge in the twentieth century.

Paul's "deconstruction" of the language of wisdom in 1 Corinthians is critical, because it establishes at many levels the terms of the debate that would dominate the coming Christian era. Returning to the text of 1 Corinthians, we should turn our attention to Paul's opening salvo against a certain type of "apologist" who apparently was well positioned at Corinth. "For Christ did not send me to baptize, but to preach the gospel—not *with wisdom and eloquence* [*sophia logou*], lest the cross of Christ be emptied of its power," Paul explains. "For the message of the cross is foolishness to those who are perishing, but to us who are being saved it is the power of God" (1 Cor 1:17-18). An early apologist for the Christian faith against pagan attacks would have naturally drawn on the common identification within Hellenistic Judaism of reason (*logos*) with wisdom (*sophia*). The identification had gone mainstream at least a century earlier with the writings of Philo of Alexandria, a respected Jewish philosopher and man of letters. The Greek words Paul invokes in this citation are telling, because they serve to relativize the importance of philosophical argument in discussions of faith, which was a sine qua non for all the Hellenizers.

Paul rattles off a string of synonyms to enforce his point about precisely whom he is describing—"the one who is wise" (*sophos*), "the scribe" (*grammateus*), "the debater" (*syzētētēs*) (ESV). The *sophos*, or wise man, was a familiar object of emulation in the Hellenistic world. Since the

Corinthians claimed to have wisdom, it is fair to assume that they were associating their view of what it means to live the Christian life with this well-recognized archetype. The Stoics viewed wisdom as a kind of emotionless detachment, leading to moral rectitude and psychological balance, which was easily filled out in the Jewish mind as a learned person who arrived at similar results through the study of Torah. The wise man enjoyed an almost godlike status in the views of ancient peoples. In other words, Stoicism was often approved by the contemporaries and immediate descendants of Paul as a largely intellectual version of Christianity. But in adding other synonyms Paul clearly intends that the reader will be led to cut his idea of the wise man down to size. The terms "scribe" and "debater" (in the Greek context we might even substitute "clerk" and "lawyer") give the word *sophos* more the sense of "sophist," the fourth-century-B.C. masters of rhetoric who had claimed they could convince anyone of anything through their art of persuasive speech and who, thanks to Socrates and the legacy of Plato, were now considered honey-tongued word sharks with no integrity or concern for genuine wisdom. The "scribe," of course, was also one of Jesus' routine targets for ridicule.

In short, Paul is saying that the prestigious philosophers of his day were nothing more than pretentious windbags. One can never be convinced by another person, no matter how eloquent they might be, of the truth of faith. The truth of faith resides elsewhere. The notion that genuine truth has to be argued or debated until one achieves wisdom through philosophy, the "love of wisdom" (*philosophia*), was the fundamental presumption of the Greek mind. But, dramatically and paradoxically, Paul in this context reduces such wisdom to stupidity or "foolishness" (*mōria*). Christ cannot be proven, only *apprehended*. He is apprehended not as human wisdom but as *God's wisdom*, a wisdom that amounts to God taking on the most wretched guise of a crucified criminal in contrast with his infinite majesty in order to overcome once and for all the purely "dialectical" opposition of finite and infinite, human language and the divine, redemptive mystery for all creation. There is no way that reason can reconcile this opposition. The cross requires simply a personal surrender *in faith* to God's mysterious workings in time and history.

One of the difficulties with the way the classical issue of faith and reason, or faith and philosophy, has been framed is that it presupposes a view of "faith" that is alien to the Hebraic context in which Paul first articulated the matter. It is true that Paul was the "apostle to the Gentiles," that he wrote in Greek, and that he used phraseology that to this day harks back to its first-century standard usage. But as biblical scholars have repeatedly emphasized, Paul was also working and writing within a Hellenistic rabbinic framework for which the Septuagint Greek translation of the Hebrew Scriptures had as much force in his thinking as the non-Judaic spin they were given in popular Hellenistic philosophy. Paul was addressing Gentiles, but he seldom quoted Greek authorities—only Jewish Scripture. His language was Hellenistic, his worldview Hebraic, which is what made Paul uniquely Paul. The misunderstanding about what Paul most likely really meant by what we translate as "faith" stems from a slight but important difference between the connotations of the Hebrew word *'ĕmûnâ* and the Greek *pistis*—a constant problem of word-for-word translation over the centuries. It also has to do with the evolution of the word *faith* in the English lexicon itself.

If faith always has primacy over philosophy, which is my position, it is because of the original meaning of the word *faith* itself in the biblical sense. The primacy of faith, enshrined in the famous insistence of the Reformation of the sixteenth century on "faith alone" (*sola fide*), was seen by the Reformers as unquestionable, because that is the theme running throughout the Bible—both the Old and New Testaments. The Hebrew *'ĕmûnâ*—from which we get "amen"—has the fundamental meaning of "trust" or "firmness" rather than "belief." When the Septuagint compilers translated it into Greek, they employed a similar term that had a respectable lineage in Hellenic thought going back to Plato. However, the difference in the grammatical environs in which the word was employed in the two languages is telling. In the Old Testament *'ĕmûnâ* had all to do with trusting God's promises, as in the case of Abraham, or in fidelity to the covenant with Yahweh in the centuries after Moses. In Plato's *Republic*, however, where the implications of the locution *pistis* (the Greek word for "faith" used throughout the New Testament) are systematically set forth for the first time, the connotations are somewhat different. Here they have more to do with what today we would describe as "common-sense" knowledge, an understanding based on what everyday experience tells us is the case or even what respected authorities have convinced us is true. It was also connected to the rhetorical art of persuasion, of which the sophists were masters, suggesting a standpoint at which we arrive after having been effectively persuaded of it. In *The Republic*, from which most ancient and even modern standards of certain knowledge ultimately derive, *pistis* is associated with views or propositions that may *seem* evident but on more careful scrutiny turn out to be wrong or misleading. Our senses or even the "common" views of ordinary people—as skeptics up until today are fond of showing—can deceive us. So can charismatic authorities or skilled orators.

For Plato, *pistis* was an inferior version of truth. It was actually the third level down from the top in a fourfold hierarchy involving grades of knowledge. In order to ensure ourselves a higher and more unshakable grasp of things, we must put our concepts to the test, seeking what the Greeks of Plato's time called *dianoia*. *Dianoia* is knowledge acquired through the comparison of opposing ideas or varying beliefs or opinions through a process known as "dialectic." Most of Plato's "dialogues," involving one or more interlocutors voicing positions that Socrates constantly challenges or refines, rely on the practice of dialectic to achieve this goal. In fact, the words *dialectic* and *dialogue* derive etymologically from the Greek *dialegein*, literally a "passing back and forth" between two or more speakers. Once we have attained *dianoia*, or comparative knowledge, we are then prepared to enjoy a true and certain way of knowing. This higher, certain knowledge Plato terms *epistēmē* (whence the contemporary word "epistemology," the theory of knowledge). *Epistēmē* is a systematic comprehension of something we have carefully thought out, often with the aid of careful philosophy instead of rhetorical arguments. *Epistēmē* takes us beyond the mere impression that something is real and genuine, leaving us with a newfound *intellectual* conviction. Hence, we note the transformative prefix *e* in the shift from *pistis* to *epistēmē*. Such conviction, however, is not the ultimate level of knowledge for Plato. That occurs when illumined thought beholds the purely rational and transcendent "forms" of things. *Epistēmē* is but a readying for what medieval Christian thinkers from Augustine onward understood as the enjoyment or contemplation of the divine, the level of pure "mind" or *nous*.

In 1 Corinthians Paul is responding within his own Hellenistic milieu to the kinds of skepticism about who Christ is—the same skepticism we encounter frequently today. Paul is offering an entirely new model of *epistēmē* that is based on faith rather than the well-known dialectical method of reasoning and argumentation. In essence, Paul refutes Plato by pushing *pistis* to the peak of the hierarchy. But he does so by making his own kind of dialectical move that is quite subtle and barely discerned by conventional biblical theologians. At one level he is reaffirming the Greek lexicology of the term *pistis* in the sense of knowledge gained by the senses or through authorities. But he is also implying that this kind of sense knowledge is completely reliable and does not require *dianoia* because it is bound up with our own personal knowledge of Christ. Furthermore, the highest "knowledge" for which the technique of *dianoia* primes us is one secured by the total surrender of our person to God's will and purpose, as well as our living in the blessed state of Christ's salvation; "we have the mind [*nous*] of Christ" (1 Cor 2:16). So far, so good. The gist of most evangelical testimonies about "faith" have to do with some profession of one's own personal experience that led us to realize that we must now rely on guidance from Christ rather than our own wants and imaginings and that we can no longer have confidence merely in our own opinions or predilections. In other words, Christ is now the authority for what we know. For Paul, this authority was founded on what he insisted was his confrontation with the risen Lord himself on the road to Damascus.

However, the encounter on the road to Damascus, for Paul, was not simply a typical experience. In the third chapter of Ephesians he characterizes it as a "revelation" (*apokalypsis*; Eph 3:3). The word *apokalypsis* (literally, "unveiling" or "laying bare") in Greek is synonymous in many respects with the word for "truth" (*alētheia*, or "unconcealedness"). The former, however, has more the connotation of an event when this unveiling takes place, the latter the state of no longer remaining hidden. Thus the truth of Christ's presence or person depends, at least in Paul's mind, on our apprehension of an event that makes a whole previously confused perspective on things somehow transparent. For Paul, what changed was his outlook on the importance of the Torah, or "law," which Jewish teaching at the time had extolled as the key to ensuring that the faithful fulfilled the unique purpose for which God had chosen them among the nations. For the Pharisee, it was the Torah that made sense of one's identity as a Jew as the living heir to God's promises to Abraham. In the previous chapter Paul refers to the spirit of revelation, or *apokalypsis*, that allows the new Christian to recognize that he now is "predestined" according to God's plan (Eph 1:11) as a Christ-follower rather than a guardian of the traditions associated with obedience to Torah. Moreover, Paul affirms that this revelation places all of human history, including the part each individual is to play in the story, in an entirely new frame of significance.

> I pray that the eyes of your heart may be enlightened in order that you may know the hope to which he has called you, the riches of his glorious inheritance in his holy people, and his incomparably great power for us who believe [*pisteuontas*]. That power is the same as the mighty strength he exerted when he raised Christ from the dead and seated him at his right hand in the heavenly realms. (Eph 1:18-20)

The "power" of what modern theologians would term the "Christ event" is what turns upside down and secures anew our faith. The event grounds both our subjective and objective faith, our confidence in what we believe (*pistis*), in this unique "revelation" that is as much about human destiny as a whole as it is about our personal righteousness. In light of this revelation, Paul says, we can now truly grasp the difference between human understanding and the "wisdom" that Christ was crucified. Because we in the modern era are accustomed to regarding the problem of faith and philosophy as a methodological challenge, or as a straightforward problem of knowledge, we fail to see how it was originally posed in the Bible itself as a broader question of *salvation*, that is, of how God will accomplish what he promised from the very beginning. In other words, as Christians we have let the legacy of Greek thought privilege the question of faith and philosophy in terms of philosophy rather than the other way around. What Paul makes clear is that philosophy itself needs to submit to the framework that God first enunciated as his pledge to Abraham. In contemporary terms, we can say that the question of faith and philosophy comes down to the question of the ultimate *meaning of history*, not the question of which epistemology, or theory of knowledge, we should rely on when we read Scripture or make decisions about our lives.

KIERKEGAARD AND THE SINGULARITY OF FAITH

The parameters of the question of the proper relationship between faith and reason itself have shifted considerably over the centuries. The Councils of Nicaea, Ephesus and Chalcedon during the waning years of the Roman Empire not only formalized the Christian creeds about the relationship between the historical man Jesus and the eternal Godhead, but also served to fix by decree the meaning and usages of certain Greek philosophical terms such as *ousia* ("substance") or *physis* ("nature") that had been employed routinely, sometimes in ambiguous ways, in articulating a common faith language for the early church. The so-called synthesis of faith and reason by St. Thomas Aquinas in the thirteenth century had a similar aim. It was motivated by the intellectual necessity of coming to terms with the fast-growing philosophical influence of Islamic philosophy, which had appropriated Greek thought by translating numerous long-lost ancient philosophical texts, especially Aristotle, and deploying them to make arguments that many Christian thinkers, complacent with now shopworn forms of Catholic dogma, found unsettling. Islamic philosophy could have been ignored were it not the long-looming military and political threat to Europe posed by the armies of the Muslim caliph. Aquinas rose to this challenge in the manner many Christian philosophers after him have done. He adopted Aristotelianism carte blanche in order to argue vigorously for the truth of the Christian faith over what he called "the pagans," which included both Greeks and Muslims.

However, since the eighteenth century exactly the same kind of challenge has come from the experimental sciences. It is the prestige of the "scientific method" that poses such a challenge. The cachet of modern science derives from two primary sources: (1) the elegance and clarity of its formulations; (2) its practical success in making sense out of many long-abiding mysteries about the natural world as a whole, as well as its "cash out" in familiar technologies that address the little, routine problems of human life and day-to-day instances of suffering. Through the creation of useful consumer technologies science also has the power to give us what we want, thereby relying on what Christians understand as our "fallen" tendency to focus on our own will rather than God's. In both obvious and not so obvious ways Christian philosophy, at least from the mid-twentieth century onward, has taken Aquinas to another level by buying into the covert assumptions of the new science and arguing for the Christian faith as if it were an equal or superior type of scientific rationality with its own kind of internal logic. The common view, particularly among Christian evangelical philosophers, that apologetics amounts to developing consistent formal procedures for demonstrating how faith statements can be turned into cogently defensible "propositions," frequently appealing to the latest and most sophisticated innovations in the philosophy of language or the philosophy of science, exemplifies this trend.

Of course, to insist on the contrary that any account of faith comes down to the meaning of history can easily be caricatured or misconstrued. History itself is inconsequential without some comprehension not only of what each and every one of us does with our own lives, but also of how what Kierkegaard dubbed one's own "eternal destiny" is decided. History is the grand ensemble of private destinies and personal biographies. God does not work out our salvation for us, unless one adheres to the strictest rendering of the Calvinist doctrine of predestination. Each of us works out our salvation in our own inimitable way, as the saying goes, "with fear and trembling" (Phil 2:12). In the early nineteenth century Søren Kierkegaard, following figures like Blaise Pascal almost two hundred years earlier, demanded that grand philosophical schemes should not chart the great meaning of history. According to Kierkegaard, such philosophical schemes are what he constantly called "absent minded," overlooking the plight of the "existing individual."[7] Sal-

---

[7]For a passage where Kierkegaard develops this argument fully, see his *Concluding Unscientific Postscript*, trans. David F. Swenson (Princeton, NJ: Princeton University Press, 1968), pp. 109-10.

vation is the immediate consequence of a personal decision, Kierkegaard demanded. It cannot be explained or logically justified through appeal to some overarching, philosophical and broadly theoretical view of how God operates in time and space. There is nothing in any philosophy of history that can persuade or encourage me to "become a Christian," which in itself is something I don't decide once and for all but in each decision I make every day. Kierkegaard described a decision to "become a Christian" as a "leap" one makes "by virtue of the absurd." In *Fear and Trembling* Kierkegaard treats the story of Abraham's response to God's summons that he climb Mount Moriah and sacrifice his son Isaac with a knife, right after the Lord himself had given Abraham a promised heir in whom the nations would be blessed, as paradigmatic of what faith in this sense entails. Kierkegaard names Abraham the "knight of faith." For Kierkegaard, "faith is the highest passion in a human being."[8] But this passion is activated through the very "paradox" in which faith consists.

> Faith is just this paradox, that the single individual as the particular is higher than the universal, is justified before the latter, not as subordinate, though in such a way . . . that it is the single individual who, having been subordinate to the universal as the particular, now by means of the universal becomes that individual who, as particular, stands in an absolute relationship to the absolute.[9]

Kierkegaard was writing against the outsize influence during his time of the German philosopher G. W. F. Hegel. In his writings, Hegel had taken the ancient Greek dialectic and turned it into a systematic means of comprehending the whole of reality, including human history. Reason reaches beyond the individual conscious subject, according to Hegel, and unfolds within an increasingly grandiose scope the interconnections among all elements of reality. Hegel's own version of the "dialectic" proceeds by thought positing its logical opposite then opposing itself to that very opposition. Whenever I say "this," for example, I automatically presuppose a "not this" or a "that." But the status of both the "this" and the "not-this" depends on the movement of thought itself, *which returns to*

---

[8]Søren Kierkegaard, *Fear and Trembling*, trans. Alastair Hannay (New York: Penguin, 1985), p. 151.
[9]Ibid., p. 64.

itself as a consciousness of their relationships as well as a moment of *self-consciousness*, in which the negative terms are held fast together through the realization of *my* relationship to them. For example, in a famous illustration often cited by different philosophers, many are not aware that the bright "evening" star we see on the horizon in the evening is from the astronomer's point of view the same as the so-called morning star. When someone informs us that these two "different" stars are one and the same, and the common name is Venus, we begin to realize that disparate experiences are now brought together into a unified concept.

Hegel considers the dialectical unfolding of thought as a three-part process, what is popularly referred to as "thesis, antithesis, synthesis" (although Hegel himself never used this particular nomenclature). The more we think about the meaning and implications of a certain idea, the more we begin to consider seriously its opposite. But as we ponder the antithetical relationship between the two ideas, we become aware of a further thought construct that combines these ideas and cancels the distinction. Hegel calls that third "moment" of thought the "negation of the negation."[10] The most familiar, and therefore critical, polarity in thought occurs when we reflect on the difference between ourselves and what is not ourselves, between consciousness and what we are *conscious of.* Prior to Hegel, Western philosophy had taken for granted this contrast between self and not-self, the so-called subject-object split. But thought also has the capacity to *think of itself*, that is, to incorporate the self itself in the idea of what the subject is thinking. Aristotle had, in fact, defined God not simply as First Cause or Prime Mover, but as "thought thinking upon itself." But thought thinking upon itself—what we might dub *pure self-consciousness*—requires far more than the reflexive recognition that I somehow *know about myself.* In order to know about myself I must grasp the intricate and concrete relationships between myself and the things in the world that I have experienced and thought about. Thus self-consciousness also involves the progressive self-reflection of all objects of thought in relationship to my evolving knowledge of myself.

Human knowledge, according to Hegel, is identified with the process

---

[10]For example, Georg Wilhelm Friedrich Hegel, *The Logic*, in *Encyclopaedia of the Philosophical Sciences*, trans. William Wallace, 2nd ed. (London: Oxford University Press, 1874), §93.

of reason and an evolving spiral of self-knowledge. It is gradually forged over time through the interconnections of multiple instances of self-understanding. The driving force of the process he called "Spirit" with a capital *S*. But Spirit is not only the superconscious impulse behind the process, it also signifies that universal, transpersonal consciousness the Christian faithful address as God. That higher consciousness becomes "conscious" of itself in the intricate instances of history where each individual consciousness progressively realizes itself in each concrete instance of the dialectical development of self-consciousness. In other words, God becomes "aware" of himself in each instance in which we as persons become aware of ourselves. Thus at some level God can be identified with human self-consciousness, but Hegel does not explicitly make such a claim. His interpreters are left to wonder whether he meant it would be the case only "in the end," that is, at some eschatological climax of history.

As far as Kierkegaard was concerned, these exceedingly authoritative views held by Hegel amounted to a type of historical pantheism, subtly leveraging the Christian idea of providence in its diverse ramifications to concoct a completely deterministic worldview in which the pathos of the existing individual is totally eclipsed by philosophical elegance and cleverness. Indeed, Hegel repeatedly suggested that philosophy is both the highest form of *self-knowledge*, not simply knowledge in the general sense, and the supreme dialectical synthesis of all moments of self-awareness. Moreover, Hegel coyly implied that the philosopher himself is like unto God. Hegel also identified the "rational" with the "real," suggesting naturally that salvation *comes through reason alone*. Hegel, in other words, though a Lutheran Christian, turned the very Lutheran principle of *sola fide* upside down.

But, for Kierkegaard, there was a different kind of "dialectic" that cannot be "taken up" (in Hegel's language) into a higher form of rational consciousness where every previous negation is somehow negated. That is the "dialectic" of individual human existence. The dialectic of individual existence consists in the projection of my own desires, aspirations and imagined possibilities into a future in which death is encountered as eventual and unavoidable. The opposition between my projected sense of self and the universal inexorability of death is impossible to overcome *dialectically*. In a direct jab at Hegel, Kierkegaard writes in his *Concluding Unscientific Postscript* that an individual acutely conscious of his mortality "also assumes to explain universal history, then it may be that what he says about universal history is glorious, but what he says about death is stupid."[11] Death cannot be philosophically comprehended or dialectically rationalized. Therefore as an "existing individual," as Kierkegaard says, I am thrown back upon my own isolation, solitude and anxiety in the face of my ultimate annihilation.

Kierkegaard's views represent the baseline argument of what would later by known as "existentialism." For all the various misuses of the term in both philosophy and popular culture over the years, existentialism means starting from the standpoint of "existence"—*my* life, *my* longings, *my* anxieties and *my* passions—rather than from some abstract premise or proposition that can be elaborated "rationally" into a set of general inferences or conclusions. Reason on the whole, and philosophical reason specifically, remains impotent when I, as an existing individual, confront the full context of who I am as a human being and what it means to be self-conscious. For Kierkegaard, existence is intimately bound up with not only mortality but also *temporality*. Mortal beings on their own cannot steel themselves against the ravages of time. Yet the object of Christian faith, Kierkegaard assures us, is a singular event in human history in which the eternal conquered the temporal. That was the coming of Christ, the "God-man" who embodies the very presence and perdurance of eternity *within time*. This event cannot be reconciled through reason. It cannot be made *real* by rational understanding. Hegel's "speculative" philosophy—a philosophy proceeding through the "mirroring" (the word comes from the Latin *speculum* for mirror) of opposites to overcome that opposition—cannot comprehend this event. The event itself is a paradox. It remains irrevocably *absurd*. Christian faith, therefore, has nothing to do with "belief" in God or any generic gesture toward acknowledging a higher being or truth. Kierkegaard revived Luther's slogan of *sola fide*, but one that did not set its face

---

[11]Kierkegaard, *Concluding Unscientific Postscript*, p. 149.

against Catholic doctrine, but against the putative Hegelian "synthesis" of faith and philosophy. It is only "by virtue of the absurd" that faith—as the very passion for eternity on the part of the existing individual—can be expressed.

Kierkegaard is usually regarded as the modern poster child for the argument that faith and philosophy are incommensurable. Although his writings were mainly targeted at a very definite intellectual adversary— Hegel, or more precisely, Hegelianism as a nineteenth-century movement out of which modern liberal theology stemmed—Kierkegaard raised, and continues to raise for us today, critical questions that were first posed by Paul and later by Tertullian. Whenever the claim is made that faith in Christ can somehow be "demonstrated" by certain, well-crafted philosophical maneuvers, Kierkegaard always functions as a reminder that there are essential and foundational difficulties with such a position. Kierkegaard was not merely a nineteenth-century Danish anti-intellectual. His own *reasoning against reason* has to be taken quite seriously. Whereas his personal biography is shot through with idiosyncrasies and what today we would probably diagnose as psychological disorders; and whereas his idea of Christianity excludes the very insistence on the importance of a faith community central not only to Paul but also to the historic church; nevertheless his rhetorical style and the cogency of what he says is overwhelming. Kierkegaard serves as an unsettling conscience for thinkers who blithely assume that what the Bible terms "faith" can be argued successfully in accordance with established philosophical procedures, even if those protocols are allegedly "Christian."

As Kierkegaard reiterates over and over through his writings, the philosophical temptation is forever to "go beyond faith," as if faith could simply be construed as one more starting point of formal reasoning or as a straightforward empirical given. There is nothing commonsensical about the incarnation. Faith and philosophy do not inhabit the same systems of signification but in many respects operate in parallel universes. The philosophical universe is made up of abstract figures or concepts, like the characters in *Flatland*.[12] Faith is profoundly

---

[12]*Flatland* is a famous satirical novel from the nineteenth century by Edwin Abbot. It focuses on how figures from one dimension (e.g., points and lines) cannot comprehend figures from two

human and "existential," because "reality . . . cannot be expressed in the language of abstraction."[13] Kierkegaard's celebrated dictum that "truth is subjectivity," found in his *Philosophical Fragments and Concluding Unscientific Postscript*,[14] should not at all be interpreted, as facile critics of him are accustomed to doing, as a manifesto of relativism. Truth is "subjective" in Kierkegaard's eyes, because faith is irremediably subjective. No one can live in faith except *myself* alone. Only *I* can experience the prospect of death. Only *I* can come to terms with the paradox, or contradiction, that Christ died for me, and then I can only do so by living my life for him. If we take Christ confessionally as "fully God and fully human," as the church fathers asserted, then only faith can make sense of that "proposition." Only *I* can make sense of it through the testimony of my own life.

THE LEGACY OF THE PROTESTANT REFORMATION

Kierkegaard's ideas are part of an enduring modern legacy, much of which stems from the Protestant Reformation of the sixteenth century. The different Protestant Reformers of that period tended to have a jaundiced eye toward rational or discursive argument about the meaning of faith, if it were not integrally anchored in the conscience and *personal* commitment of the individual believer. The Reformers were deeply suspicious of all efforts to "rationalize" faith, because they believed that reason had been corrupted and distorted by the original sin of Adam, in keeping with Paul's famous characterization of the human condition in Romans 1: "For although they knew God, they neither glorified him as God nor gave thanks to him, but their thinking became futile and their foolish hearts were darkened. Although they claimed to be wise, they became fools" (Rom 1:21-22).

The Reformers' *existential* grounding of faith in a deep consciousness of sin and a personal surrender to the saving power of the gospel proceeded hand in hand with their uncompromising insistence that every

---

dimensions (e.g., squares and circles). Furthermore, the same holds for two-dimensional beings when confronting those from the third dimension (as when a circle encounters a sphere). See Edwin Abbot, *Flatland: A Romance of Many Dimensions* (New York: Dover, 1992).

[13]Ibid., p. 279.

[14]Kierkegaard, *Concluding Unscientific Postscript*, p. 178.

Christian read the Bible for himself and shape his life around the authority of what he understood, plainly and simply, as "God's Word." *Sola fide* ("faith alone") was intimately bound up in their minds with *sola Scriptura* (the authority of "Scripture alone"). It was chiefly for this reason that Martin Luther, the instigator and original architect of the Protestant Reformation, dismissed philosophical disputation about matters of faith as "harlotry" and referred to reason as "a great whore."[15] His motivations were fairly evident. The allusions in his rhetoric were not only to the figure of the "whore of Babylon" in the book of Revelation but also to the Roman Catholic Church itself, which he identified with that notorious Biblical archetype. The Reformation was all about the standpoint from which one could "live by faith." The church, generally speaking, had taught for centuries that an uninformed and unreasoned personal faith was merely "implicit" and had to be made *explicit* through gradually cognizing and acknowledging the official pronouncements of the pope, the councils and the ordained clergy, who often relied on their own official "philosophers" to interpret the subtle meanings of points of doctrine. Since Scripture often was incidental to the cumulative conclusions of previous authorities, the Reformers found that the so-called classical "Thomistic" synthesis of faith and philosophy (based on the writings of Thomas Aquinas in the thirteenth century) had been grossly abused by subordinating God's revealed truth to the opinions of human beings.

Protestantism sought to take the rational methodologies of philosophy more seriously once the scientific revolution got underway in the seventeenth century. Ironically, the emergence of modern science was concentrated in the new Protestant countries such as England and Germany, a complex process that has fascinated historians of ideas for over a century now. However, as the same scholars have consistently pointed out, the new empirical and mathematical sciences did not arise *directly* from the Protestant emphasis on the priority of faith but because of its neglect of "natural reason." The earlier medieval attitude that nature and Scripture were one seamless tapestry that philosophy was enticed to explore prevented Catholic thinkers from investigating physical phenomena on

---

[15]For example, see Martin Luther, *Luther's Works: Sermons I*, ed. and trans. John W. Doberstein (Philadelphia: Muhlenberg Press, 1958), 51:374.

their own terms rather than through the distorted lens of dogma. The example of Galileo, who was forced to recant his discoveries about the nature of planetary motion because they contradicted official clerical doctrine, is the most well-known illustration of this tendency. Because Protestants with their exclusive concentration on the primacy of biblical knowledge were inclined to treat nature not as "sacred" but as irrelevant to salvation itself, they were free to construct scientific hypotheses and experiments free of church interference. That all changed two centuries later with Darwin, but that is an entirely different story.[16]

Protestant theologians such as John Calvin held that the "natural reason" was a suitable method in which to discover God's beneficent and providential workings throughout time and history, but he did not regard it as a significant intellectual preoccupation. Calvin maintained that such pursuits should be focused on a "revealed knowledge" that can be acquired solely in the study of God's Word. In his *Institutes of the Christian Religion*, first published in Latin in 1559 and in French a year later, Calvin asserted that through the pursuit of science we only attain "knowledge of God the Creator." Through the theological study of Scripture we arrive, nevertheless, at "knowledge of God the Redeemer." Following Augustine's *Confessions*, Calvin also gave priority to self-knowledge, a constant spiritual and moral inventory that discloses our own finitude and sinfulness. In the *Institutes* Calvin developed what came to be known as the *duplex cognitio Dei*, the "double knowledge of God." We can only share in the redemptive knowledge that Jesus Christ is our savior once we have thoroughly scrutinized our failings and our essential need for salvation. "In order to apprehend God," Calvin wrote, "it is unnecessary to go farther than ourselves."[17] Therefore, natural knowledge is irrelevant to our ultimate concern, which should be about our relationship with God and our heavenly salvation.

Paradoxically, it is the Protestant emphasis on self-knowledge and personal redemption that has made it historically resistant to the ancient

---

[16]This general argument was first laid out in detail by E. A. Burtt in *The Metaphysical Foundations of Modern Science* (New York: Dover, 2003), but it has been developed elsewhere by other intellectual historians as well.

[17]John Calvin, *Institutes of the Christian Religion*, trans. Henry Beveridge (Peabody, MA: Hendrickson, 2008), 1.5.3.

idea of *credo ut intelligam* ("I believe, so that I may understand") or *fides quaerans intellectum* ("faith seeking understanding") that were formulated by the church fathers, particularly Augustine, in late antiquity. Even such an important modern philosopher as the eighteenth-century thinker Immanuel Kant sought to restrict the domain of "pure reason" to what he termed the "practical" or "moral" deliberations of the subjective will, while at the same time rejecting what he dismissed as "speculative" or "theoretical" considerations about the nature of the universe that had nothing to do with his two overriding questions: "what ought I to do?" and "for what can I hope?" Kantian subjectivism in some guise or another has dominated Protestant thought since the sixteenth century, and it is only with the very strange marriage of Anglo-American analytical philosophy and Protestant orthodoxy in America since the 1970s that evangelical thought, in particular, has taken the dubious step of trying to be "objective" and "scientific" in its approach to faith.

As I have noted in detail in my book *The Next Reformation*, it is even more peculiar that Protestant orthodoxy has embraced as its preferred method of "apologetics" that very approach. The approach was actually first propounded by militant atheists such as Bertrand Russell at the beginning of the twentieth century and extensively invoked during the next hundred years by the Anglo-American philosophical establishment either to discredit or to minimize the importance of Christian faith.[18] As Michael Levine has wryly observed, this pandering to the intellectual enemies of faith—a Mephistophelean bargain, to say the least—in the fatuous belief that somehow it will serve to convince nonbelievers of their errors is "indicative of its lack of vitality, relevance, and 'seriousness.'"[19] If the new pseudo-"synthesis" of faith and reason arising out of the "irrelevance" of Christian, analytic, evangelical philosophy serves to renounce its own vigorous Protestant heritage, at the same time, it unwittingly makes its own unintended pact with the devil by seeking to demonstrate logically the "truth" of certain confessional propositions.

---

[18]See Carl Raschke, *The Next Reformation: Why Evangelicals Must Embrace Postmodernity* (Grand Rapids: Baker Academic, 2004).

[19]Michael Levine, "Christian Analytic Philosophy of Religion," in *Faith and Reason: Friends or Foes in the New Millennium*, ed. Anthony Fisher and Haydon Ramsey (Adelaide, Australia: ATF Press, 2004), pp. 134-52.

What kinds of arguments remain, then, to retain the vitality of the tradition, running back through Luther to Paul, that gives primacy to faith alone (*sola fide*)? There are naturally still some important options.

POSTMODERNISM AND THE "NEXT REFORMATION"

The key may lie in a distinctive philosophical revolution that began soon after World War II in France and spread across most of Europe and swept into America during the last quarter century of the old millennium. That revolution has been vaguely named "postmodernism" and has been thoroughly misunderstood as well as obtusely and ignorantly attacked by its critics, who habitually associate it with something equally thin, vaporous and obscure they rhetorically call "relativism." Postmodernism as a philosophical movement historically *has nothing to do with relativism.* Until its critics dare to confront the fact that they are systematically abusing and distorting the meaning of technical terms, which of course is quite odd as a whole for analytic philosophers, there can be no serious discussion. The negative judgment is presupposed in the false premises that are advanced from the outset, comparable to the long-standing and infamous question, Have you stopped beating your wife yet? The question of course presupposes one is beating his wife, which may very well not be true at all. To describe a cultural phenomenon—and unthinking and uncritical forms of relativistic sentimentality such as "it's true if it's true for me" or "everyone's view is equally valid" have indeed been around for a long time—critics are entitled to use whatever terms they wish. But the philosophical language and stances of certified "postmodern" philosophers themselves cannot by any stretch of the imagination be termed "relativistic."

The origins of relativism ironically can be traced to the positions of the founders of analytical philosophy themselves, such as G. E. Moore, Ludwig Wittgenstein, Gottlieb Frege and of course Bertrand Russell. They center on the somewhat dogmatic view of these thinkers that while "statements of fact" can be successfully argued through inferential reasoning and rationally demonstrated, religious questions, or "value-claims," are merely subjective expressions of "preference" or "feeling." About the same time that early analytical philosophy was demolishing the historical house of Plato and Kant by denying categorically any "rational basis" to faith or morality, social scientists—and anthropologists especially—were documenting numerous distinctive cultures or social groupings with conflicting, and seemingly equally cogent, value systems and types of moral behavior. The notion of "moral equivalency," the idea that any religious or moral standpoint compares favorably with any other, was anchored as one of the bedrock assumptions of relativism, because it seemingly could be validated through empirical observation. By and large analytical philosophy, aside from its adoption by Christian apologists, has continued to stress in different ways the problematic, or ambiguous, nature of faith claims. There still remains, therefore, an internal inconsistency between how the methodology pioneered by Russell and Wittgenstein is utilized, often to contradictory ends, by Christian and secular philosophers.

Analytical philosophy, as many of its critics without theological interests have stressed over the years, has certain built-in limitations that confine its plausible operations primarily to general questions in the philosophy of science or *modern epistemology*—the theory of how knowledge as a whole is reliably obtained and responsibly evaluated. These limitations are one of the main reasons that in the last quarter century philosophers with deeper concerns about the significance and vital role of faith have turned away from analytical methods and put their arms around the more conceptually abstract and historically grounded tradition that has come to be called "Continental thought" (in order to distinguish it from its Anglo-American counterparts). So-called postmodern philosophy, with a few exceptions, tends to be thoroughly Continental. Continental philosophy today is an ongoing and fluid amalgam primarily of German idealism, French structuralism and "poststructuralism," and phenomenology. Since the end of the 1980s the Continental strain of philosophy has taken a decided "religious turn," as the Dutch thinker Hent de Vries first phrased it.[20] Most of the serious and "relevant" philosophical discussions of faith issues today tend to be framed within the Continental tradition. When it comes to discussions, unfortunately,

---

[20]See Hent de Vries, *Philosophy and the Turn to Religion* (Baltimore: Johns Hopkins University Press, 1999).

Continental and analytical philosophers are like cats and dogs, fierce genetic rivals that usually hiss and spit at each other but occasionally do reach some kind of amity or modus vivendi.

What makes Continental thought, and its subset "postmodernism," persuasive is not that it is dominated by French and German representatives, but that it tends to be far more literate about and loyal to the historic Western tradition, considering classical figures such as Descartes, Leibniz and Kant still highly consequential for addressing the ongoing "problems" of philosophy. Analytical philosophy, on the other hand, while giving lip service to the tradition, tends to assume that questions of logic and language are the only remaining relevant concerns for the tradition since the revolution started by Russell and Wittgenstein came into full bloom.

At the same time postmodern philosophy has preserved methodologically the analytical preoccupation with questions of language while altering the entire paradigm of how meaning and signification function overall in philosophical discourse. It is this nuanced and more sophisticated understanding of language itself that allows postmodern Continental thinkers to navigate successfully the tricky passages between existential faith commitments and considerations about valid and general rules of inference. *Postmodernism* as a philosophical, rather than a cultural, term was actually a more general label slapped on a somewhat esoterically named movement in French thought during the mid-1980s. That term was *poststructuralism*, used throughout the 1960s and 1970s to describe the innovations in theories of language and meaning developed as the so-called second wave of what the French at the time called *structural linguistics*. Structural and poststructural linguistics offered profound insights about how language functions in the real world, including in the arts, morality, politics and religion by developing a model that analytical philosophy in its preoccupation with scientific methods of investigation and verification entirely ignored or ruled out of court.

"Postmodernism" was originally nothing more than an original and compelling theory of discourse founded on actual observations and analysis of both written and spoken languages. In that respect it was more "scientific" than analytical philosophy (which had already taken years earlier what was called "the linguistic turn") actually was in practice. The new "linguistic" approach in early postmodern philosophy had three central foci. First, it recognized that the meaning of statements or propositions cannot be separated from the entire text in which they are embedded and that reading texts in order to figure out what they are really saying is just as important as ascertaining if they are logically coherent or verifiable through empirical testing. All texts are located within an intelligible *context*, but this context can only be determined through rereading, comparison with other texts and interpretation of what has been said. Meaning is ultimately determined by how the intricate structures of communication work together in an overarching manner, and it is up to the interpreter to provide a new framework of discourse in which what was first written or spoken can be fleshed out. The "truth" of a text can be discerned in its *deployability* within a particular set of life circumstances.

This principle makes postmodern readings of biblical texts dependent on the way they inspire faith in the believer and how one lives out that faith, what the medieval exegetes referred to as its *applicatio* (or "application"). The principle is not unlike what Kierkegaard had in mind when he insisted that the "truth" of faith does not lie in its propositional certainty but in the way it elicits *passion* in the person of faith. The suggestion of Derrida, postmodernity's most important philosopher, that the passion of faith, like the longing for justice, is eminently "undeconstructible" implies that such truths are existential rather than simply propositional.

Propositional logic, whether exercised for the clarification of terms in a formal argument or to prove the validity of some simple assertion, is inadequate to make sense out of the "revealed" truth of Scripture for one compelling reason: it speaks to the disinterested intellect, whereas God through his Word speaks to the whole person, including the human heart and what in both ancient Greek and later Christian philosophy is known as *synderesis*, or "conscience." The concept of *synderesis* can be found in the New Testament and plays a major role not only in late Stoic philosophy but also in writings of the church fathers and medieval Christian thinkers. Moreover, the Reformers put it at the forefront of their critique of Roman Catholic scholasticism and in forging what they understood as a genuine "evangelical" theology. It is their *synderesis* that, according to Paul, serves a spark of conscience through which, as the Reformers put it, one has an innate or "natural" knowledge of God, whereby they are "without excuse" whenever they behold the creation and still act in a depraved manner (Rom 1:19-23).

But more important, it is *synderesis*, as Christian moral philosophers from Bonaventure in the twelfth century to Kant in the eighteenth century have insisted, that serves as the faculty of discernment not merely as to what is right and wrong but also as to what is God's will in any given situation. Kant himself termed this faculty "practical reason," and maintained that its principles cannot be demonstrated discursively but only in terms of the fidelity and consistency of our ethical behavior. The Reformed tradition, furthermore, ties conscience (*synderesis*) directly to our capacity to make sense of "supersensible" forms of knowledge imparted to us through divine revelation. *Synderesis* gives us access to the knowledge of God where propositional reason falters. Conscience preserves us from drawing those kinds of "ignorant" conclusions for which human argumentation is fully outfitted (i.e., the mechanisms of persuasive self-deception that Sigmund Freud dubbed "rationalization") and prompts us to the humility and self-surrender to God that makes faith possible. "For how can the human mind," Calvin writes, "measure off the measureless essence of God according to his own little measure, a mind as yet unable to establish for certain the nature of the sun's body, though men's eyes daily gaze upon it."[21]

Postmodern thought, like Reformation thought, recognizes the inherent finitude and fallibility of propositional reasoning, thereby permitting faith to proceed confidently where discursive demonstration is ill-equipped to venture. "Deconstruction" is an often quoted, while much maligned and widely misunderstood, expression in Derrida's philosophy. Deconstruction does not relativize the terms of the debate but shows their inherent limitations. It does not refer to a critical "taking apart" of truth claims and therefore neutralizing their meaning, as the word is

---

[21]Calvin, *Institutes of the Christian Religion,* trans. Ford Lewis Battles (Philadelphia: Westminster, 1960), 1.3.1.

often misconstrued; it refers to a recognition that reading and interpretation of texts force us to let go of what we regarded as straightforward, obvious and fixed meanings. Deconstruction is not an active intervention of the interpreter but automatically *happens* as we read and find the peculiar application of the text at our disposal. In the latter half of his career Derrida, who died in 2004, turned to the question of faith itself as the centerpiece of any "deconstructive" philosophy. Faith, as well as what we call reason, are not incompatible but belong to separate orders of significance. Derrida proposes this bold strategy in his groundbreaking essay "Faith and Knowledge," published in the mid-1990s. Faith, like law, is a "performative" event which "cannot belong to the set that it founds, inaugurates, or justifies." It "cannot be contained in any traditional opposition, for example that between reason and mysticism."[22]

Faith is neither irrational nor *suprarational.* It has nothing to do with "reason," per se. Faith, Derrida asserts, is simply a *response* to a divine promise, as should be familiar to us in the story of Abraham. And "promissory" statements cannot be logically validated. Promises are peculiar types of "speech acts," as the American philosopher John Searle labeled them.[23] They are validated only when they are eventually carried out, or invalidated when we fail to live up to them. One can only "trust" in or keep promises. The promise itself is not subject to immediate observation and experimentation. The "certification" of the promise consists in an *act of will*, or a decision, that determines its outcome.

As a Jew rather than as a Christian, Derrida understood that the Bible ultimately has little to do with a "logical" or "propositional" sequence of terms. A dialogue of Plato may consist of an extended "dialectical" argument, but biblical passages consist either of divine commandments or narratives that testify to God's own declarations and deeds as well as personal dealings with those who believe in and follow him. God does not speak in syllogisms or make philosophical claims that require the fallible human intellect to demonstrate them. The Bible overall, as Luther pointed

---

[22]Jacques Derrida, "Faith and Knowledge," in *Acts of Religion*, ed. Gil Anidjar (New York: Routledge, 2002), p. 57.

[23]See John R. Searle, *Speech Acts: An Essay in the Philosophy of Language* (New York: Cambridge University Press, 1970).

out tirelessly, is an affidavit of God's promises and of his faithful promise *keeping*. Saint Paul made such a case in his epistle to the Romans, where he argued exhaustively that it is only faith in God's promises that "justifies" us in the Lord's eyes. The ultimate evidence that God is good to his promises consists in Christ's coming, his death and his resurrection.

FAITH IS NOT "RATIONAL" BUT RELATIONAL

Derrida characterizes the "fiduciary" character of faith—the keeping of a solemn promise on God's part which human beings are obliged to imitate *by their own faithfulness*—as what makes it impervious to propositional or dialectical reasoning. At the altar my spouse can only evaluate my solemn promise that I will love and cherish her until death do us part in light of the fact that I deeply love her and that she believes she can trust me to do what I say. I may fall out of love with her down the line, break my vows, have an affair and in the end divorce her. However, if I do break my vows, it is not because they were "unreasonable," but because I did not persevere or remain "faithful" to her. In other words, if I break my vows, she may protest that I did not really mean what I said at the outset. Yet her objections have only to do with my intent and my good character and nothing at all to do with my talents for making a persuasive claim. I can make a persuasive claim that she should marry me based on facts and circumstances when I propose to her, but whether I turn out to be a good husband rests entirely on my *performance*. That is why Scripture says that we "recognize" someone only by the "fruits" of their actions (see Mt 7:16).

Faith, hence, is in the final analysis not rational but *relational*. What does this contention imply philosophically? There is no such thing as a "relational proposition," unless one of course is talking about a marriage proposal. The common coinage of reason is propositions. The currency of faith is promises along with deeds to show that one is attempting to keep them. That is the genuine import of the well-known and frequently misinterpreted passage in the book of James: "Show me your faith without deeds, and I will show you my faith by my deeds" (Jas 2:18). "Keeping the faith" from the standpoint not only of the Great Commandment to love God and to love our neighbor but also of Jesus' call that we "take up our cross" and follow him rests on the *quality of our relation-*

ships. From an evangelical Christian perspective, the supreme criterion of whether we have been "reborn" as Christ followers is whether we can attest to having an abiding "personal relationship" with Jesus himself. That relationship is the "proof" of our faith.

The classical approach to connecting faith and philosophy was bound up with the supposition that faith is inherently an "unformed" or "uninformed" species of knowledge, as suggested in the initial connotation of the word *pistis*, that must be clarified or "filled out" through rational inquiry. Therefore "faith seeks understanding." It was never assumed that understanding needs to seek faith. But the biblical viewpoint, in which all Christian theology at some level is moored and sustained, is rooted in the conviction that understanding *does* perpetually require increased faith, if God's ways which are not ours are not be trivialized or reduced to our own proud beliefs or fallible predictions. "Science" deals with the world at hand, and what we can deduce will happen in the future by extrapolating from what we understand as the state of things with which we are somehow familiar.

Faith is forever seeking understanding. That is what Christian philosophers from ancient times all the way through the modern era have contended in one form or another. But faith, regarded as a distinctive and *singular* personal relationship each one of us in our own way has with the living God of all times, always must lead the way. The procedures for philosophy were established two and a half millennia ago among the civilizations along the northern coast of the Mediterranean. They were formulated around the rules of dialectical argument, a method peculiar to the Indo-European family of languages with its propositional structures of grammar. In the Indo-European languages, which include such diverse tongues as Greek, Latin, German, French and English, the subject of a sentence is always joined with a string of predicates. One part of a proposition always logically entails the other. The assumption, therefore, that truth is inherently "propositional"—the operative principle of Western strategies of philosophical argument—is a kind of linguistic parochialism that Derrida dubbed our "white mythology."[24] Other lan-

---

[24]See Jacques Derrida, *Margins of Philosophy*, trans. Alan Bass (Chicago: University of Chicago Press, 1982), pp. 207-72.

guages, such as Hebrew, in which God first revealed himself, are struc-
tured in such a manner that certain terms *express* the hidden meanings
of those that have gone before them. In other words, they are based on
a *mutual relationality* among the different elements in a sentence. This
relationality cannot be easily contained within the propositional or "dialectical" architecture of philosophical argument.

Faith, regarded as a relation founded on a trust in God's goodness and
the wisdom of his ways, opens our understanding to things we cannot
necessarily anticipate or understand from the propositional perspective.
That is because God's perspective is infinite and timeless. Ours is finite
and time-bound. It is the fact of *temporality*, as the twentieth-century
philosopher Heidegger remarked, that renders knowledge eminently
uncertain. We can only meet temporality head-on through faith in the
One who has authority over all the world and mastery over all of time.
"For the LORD is good and his love endures forever; / his faithfulness
continues through all generations" (Ps 100:5).

From the simple standpoint of faith—what C. S. Lewis called "mere
Christianity"—we recognize that philosophical reason is always a sup-
plement to, not a substitute for, faith. Christian philosophy in general,
and postmodern philosophy in particular, has focused on the way in
which philosophical reason discloses its own inherent limitations. We
live from day to day in what one contemporary philosopher has termed
the "prison house of language."[25] Philosophy can call routine attention
to these prison walls and thus explode the arrogance and pretension of
those who believe they can "say it all" or "know it all." But, like Paul, we
as Christian philosophers must within that prison house of language
become "prisoners for Christ" (see Philem 1). The infinite glory and ra-
diance of God in Christ shines through the words we have been given.
As Paul himself wrote from a Roman prison, it was only within those
walls that he had come to understand "the mystery of Christ." To his
readers he proclaimed: "you will be able to understand my insight into
the mystery of Christ, which was not made known to people in other
generations as it has now been revealed by the Spirit to God's holy

---

[25]See Frederic Jameson, *The Prison-House of Language: A Critical Account of Structuralism and Russian Formalism* (Princeton, NJ: Princeton University Press, 1972).

apostles and prophets" (Eph 3:4-5). Plato said that philosophy begins in wonder, but Paul tells us that it comes down to the exposition of the "mystery," that mystery that the Word became flesh and dwelt among us. Philosophy today, once it embraces in humility its own limitations and the great mystery of which it is charged with making a modicum of sense, can serve its own "apostolic" role in dealing with the "Gentiles," as Paul conceived it. It is this tension between clarity and mystery that sustains the tension throughout the generations between faith and philosophy. We know we cannot serve two masters, because we know who our true master happens to be.

Faith Seeking Understanding Response

Alan G. Padgett

IN THIS INTERESTING CHAPTER FROM a fellow philosopher and Christian, Carl Raschke represents the noble tradition of Continental philosophy well, especially in its postmodern French mode. The chapter campaigns for a tension between faith and philosophy and does so with admirable rhetorical elegance. In keeping with Carl Raschke's philosophical approach, I have opted for a more Continental type of response than in my conversation with Boyd. Instead of an analytic approach, I will take up a conversation around classical texts by some of the great theologians and philosophers treated in CRC (as I shall refer to "Carl Raschke's Chapter" throughout). Much of French philosophy today is done through interaction with the great texts from the past.[1] My response will do the same.

My goal in this exchange will be to forward a case, *pace* CRC, that there is a proper place for what Kierkegaard called "Christian speculation" (i.e., Christian theology or Christian philosophy), what Paul called "the renewal of the mind" in Christ (Rom 12:3 NRSV) and what Luther named "right reason" (*recta ratio*). In doing so, I want to say I greatly appreciate and agree with many of the contributions this chapter makes, and indeed I have learned a good deal from Raschke's often subtle and learned books in the past.[2] Alas, this chapter does not quite live up to the quality I find in his other works, and tends to present a one-sided view too often to be fully acceptable to philosophers and historians.

TO BEGIN

CRC begins with a bold thesis. "For most of the last two thousand years,"

---

[1]Alain Badiou, a philosopher but not a Christian, has written a fascinating study of Paul, which provides one example of this trend: *St. Paul: The Foundation of Universalism* (Stanford: Stanford University Press, 2003).

[2]See, for example, his early book *Alchemy of the Word: Language and the End of Theology*, AAR Studies in Religion (Missoula, MT: Scholars Press, 1979), or more recently, *The Next Reformation: Why Evangelicals Must Embrace Postmodernity* (Grand Rapids: Baker Academic, 2004).

we are told, "Christian faith" and "philosophy" have been "in tension" (p. 35). This invites us into a one-sided and sweeping narrative that ignores alternative voices in the tradition, even majority voices in some cases. Complex issues from the past (such as the relationship between Judaism and Hellenism) are in fact more subtle and historically complex that one would surmise from reading CRC. There is real tension and sometimes conflict in the story of faith and reason, or in formal terms, Christian theology and pagan philosophy: but to overemphasize tension obfuscates the larger picture and caricatures the historical reality. Of course some elements of rationality are rightly rejected, in different ways, by Christian theologians and philosophers and theologians over the centuries. But this is hardly the main thrust or always the major voice of the Christian tradition.[3] Thomas Aquinas is an obvious counterexample to CRC's main point, but is dismissed as achieving nothing more than a "*so-called* synthesis between faith and reason" (p. 47, my emphasis). In my view, using a *reasoning based on faith* and illumined by the grace of the Holy Spirit can be an important part of our discipleship in the world. I will argue, briefly, that Paul, Luther and Kierkegaard agree with this view, despite what one might glean from CRC.

On the other hand, there is a more nuanced sense of "tension" explicated at the end of CRC, and here I find a possibility of agreement with at least the view I just mentioned. It is well put, as is much of CRC, and deserves to be quoted in full (p. 67).

> Philosophy today, once it embraces in humility its own limitations and the great mystery of which it is charged with making a modicum of sense, can serve its own "apostolic" role in dealing with the "Gentiles," as Paul conceived it. It is this tension between clarity and mystery that sustains the tension throughout the generations between faith and philosophy. We know we cannot serve two masters, because we know who our true master happens to be.

This last paragraph holds open the door for a humble and faithful place for Christian wisdom and a redeemed reason in either philosophy

---

[3]I speak from experience, having coauthored with Colin Brown and Steve Wilkens a three-volume history of *Christianity and Western Thought* (Downers Grove, IL: IVP Academic, 1990-2009). Brown covers the classical and medieval period in vol. 1, while I tackled postmodernity in vol. 3.

or theology. The degree to which this is realized remains to be seen, but as Raschke is also the author of *The End of Theology*, I may be hoping for too much.[4] What is clear is that CRC presses for tension between reason and belief, sometimes with admirable subtlety and nuance. However, too often CRC presents a one-sided history, overemphasizing conflict between philosophical reason and saving faith.

JEW-GREEK: READING THE WHOLE BIBLE

The story of the tension between "Jew" and "Greek" in Raschke is the story of the complex relationship between biblical religion and pagan philosophy. Many of the historical details in CRC on this point are painted with rather too broad a brush, and presented in a way that emphasizes "tension" while bypassing what does not fit into this emphasis.[5] Even in a chapter written for a broad audience there is space for subtlety, and no reason to be one-sided. The above quotation from CRC makes this obvious, if it was not so before! However, there was in fact just as much union, discussion and synergy between biblical faith and Hellenistic reason as there was tension. This applies not only to the Bible itself but also to the long and fascinating love-hate affair between Judaism and Hellenism. For example, CRC bypasses the powerful theme of *godly wisdom* in the Bible, a wisdom that begins with the "fear of the Lord," that is, with true obedience to the law and will of God.

Of course the Bible rejects worldly wisdom or an unbalanced quest for knowledge apart from love (1 Cor 8:1-3); these lead to idolatry or poor discipleship. But the Bible taken as a whole does not reject *all* wisdom, knowledge and understanding. There is a place, but not the central place, for the mind as part of a whole person-in-community, as we all seek to follow Jesus. In the words of Paul, as Christians we seek to "take every thought captive to the obedience of Christ" (2 Cor 10:5 NASB).

In the New Testament, CRC overlooks the wisdom teachings of Jesus and the main book of Christian wisdom, the letter of James. Still, a short

---

[4]Carl Raschke, *The End of Theology* (Aurora, CO: Davies Group, 2000). This is his update of *Alchemy of the Word* cited above.
[5]An outstanding, careful and well-documented history of this relationship is found in Martin Hengel, *Judaism and Hellenism*, 2 vols. (Philadelphia: Fortress, 1974), with particular attention to Palestine.

chapter cannot cover everything, so we can understand this focus on one apostle, namely Paul. But even on Paul, the presentation errs in favor of a kind of Christian antireason. One of the strengths of CRC is a long discussion of several texts by Paul. Paul certainly argued against the pretensions of "worldly wisdom," or any use of the mind that sets itself up against Christ and the gospel. But for Paul it is equally true that the mind has a role to play in true discipleship.

In the light of faith in Christ and all God has done for us, Paul could write to the Romans, "Do not be conformed to this age, but be transformed by the renewal of your mind [*nous*], that you may approve of that which is the will of God: what is good, well-pleasing and mature" (Rom 12:2, my translation). Paul had a real place for the discipleship of our mind, too, and did not simply reject any and all use of human reason. He was very concerned that the quest for knowledge in and of itself could undermine true obedience and faith. Yet CRC overlooks the fact that for Paul, Christians have "the mind of Christ" and so we do preach "a message of wisdom among the mature [believers]" (1 Cor 2:6, 16 NIV). While discussion of Scripture is essential, I would have preferred a much more robust affirmation of the place of reason in the life of faith in CRC.

ON LUTHER

Luther's theology was in certain ways a long commentary on the epistles of Paul. He was a powerful rhetorician and often an acidic opponent in his writings, exaggerating and name-calling from time to time. Reading only his negative, passionate rejection of "Reason" and "Aristotle," one would not know of his deep knowledge and use of medieval logic and philosophy or his appreciation of redeemed reason based on Christ. The various and diverse texts we have by Luther present almost contradictory, and certainly very different, sayings about reason. The historian Brian Gerrish helpfully distinguished between three uses of the term "reason" (*ratio*) in Luther: natural reason, arrogant and sinful reason, and "regenerate reason, serving humbly in the household of faith, but always subject to the Word of God."[6]

---

[6] B. A. Gerrish, *Grace and Reason* (Oxford: Clarendon, 1962), p. 26.

Among his many works, it is especially in his theological disputations and discussion of various "theses" and his discussion and defense of the doctrines of Christ and of the sacraments that Luther most readily embraced and incorporated medieval philosophy and logic, especially what we now call the "nominalist" school. Luther certainly saw human reason as the activity of a whole person, one that can be corrupted and corrupting of others when controlled by sin in us; but this faculty could be useful as a tool or source of understanding when grounded in Christ and the gospel. It was in this positive mood that he once wrote, "compared to other things in this life, it [reason] is the best and something divine."[7] The best place to study Luther as philosopher is in his various disputations rather than in his polemical dismissals of reason in some texts when he was thinking of "reason" as sinful and controlled by human pride.[8]

ON KIERKEGAARD

We turn now to Kierkegaard in our necessarily brief response.[9] Faith is understood by him as a radical trust (he was a Lutheran), as an individualistic "leap of faith" into the absurd, as an existentially powerful trust in Christ that is nonrational and beyond reason. Faith as radical trust can be given testimony, but never fully demonstrated nor proved by logic or science, as CRC says. For Kierkegaard, the incarnation (and I would add from my perspective, the cross) is a radically antirationalist reality, an absolute paradox that shatters philosophical or scientific pretensions to know God through pure reason.

That this radical personal *trust* is a powerful element of genuine saving faith we can and should accept. We should follow Kierkegaard in seeing this leap of faith as beyond reason, however much reason may lead up to it in the life of someone like C. S. Lewis. Some truths that

---

[7]Martin Luther, "Disputation on Man," in *Luther's Works: Career of the Reformer IV*, ed. Helmut T. Lehmann and Lewis W. Spitz (Philadelphia: Fortress, 1960), 34:137.

[8]See further Theodor Dieter, "Martin Luther's Understanding of 'Reason,'" *Lutheran Quarterly* 25 (2011): 249-78, and more fully the excellent monograph by Graham White, *Luther as Nominalist: A Study of the Logical Methods Used in Martin Luther's Disputations in the Light of Their Medieval Background* (Helsinki: Luther-Agricola-Society, 1994).

[9]My interpretation of Kierkegaard is much in debt to the work of C. Stephen Evans. See in particular his volume of collected essays, *Kierkegaard on Faith and the Self* (Waco, TX: Baylor University Press, 2006).

are absolutely essential to Christian life *cannot* be demonstrated on rational and scientific grounds alone. I would put in that camp the Trinity, a full incarnation, the bodily resurrection of Jesus and other fundamental Christian truth claims. Can we give some reasons for these? To be sure we can and do! But *proof* is beyond common human reason and public evidence.

Yet even for Kierkegaard, whose many pseudonyms make straight-forward analysis difficult, the ultimate paradox of the incarnation is just that: a paradox, *not a logical contradiction*. This is important, because any sentence that contradicts itself logically must be false. We Christians testify to *truth*, do we not? Fortunately, Kierkegaard did not think of the absolute paradox as a logical contradiction, as he makes clear in *Practice in Christianity*.[10] We must be careful to understand what Kierkegaard means by "contradiction," a term that in his usage is often something more like "incongruity" or "comic absurdity."[11] The sphere of faith alone grasps the absolute paradox of Christianity, and to seek to prove it through logical means or rational understanding is an error, according to Kierkegaard.

But there is more in this great Christian philosopher's thinking about reason. Like Luther and Paul, Kierkegaard also allowed that logic and "speculation" (i.e., academic philosophy) *can* be useful to the believer and the church. To be sure, he focuses on little more than understanding the *limits* of understanding when it comes to that radical trust in Christ.[12] Christian reasoning or philosophy accepts faith in the absolute paradox as a presupposition that can never be rationally demonstrated but that

---

[10]Note the many meanings of "contradiction" here: Søren Kierkegaard, *Practice in Christianity*, trans. H. V. Hong and E. Hong (Princeton, NJ: Princeton University Press, 1991), pp. 124-27.

[11]See Evans, *Kierkegaard*, pp. 117-32.

[12]"I, if I am to understand, can neither before nor afterward come to understand anything else except that it [the absolute paradox of Christ] goes against all thinking." Søren Kierkegaard, *Concluding Unscientific Postscript*, trans. H. V. Hong and E. Hong (Princeton, NJ: Princeton University Press, 1992), 1:578. One can in the light of Christ *understand* the limits of human understanding by using reason: but philosophical reason or "speculation" cannot grasp the profound reality of Christ. When it tries to, it simply turns Christianity into some "analogy of paganism" (p. 579). Yet even Climacus can agree that a "Christian speculation" can be legitimate, as long as it accepts this paradox *as a sheer presupposition*, and does not seek to philosophically make sense of it in rational terms. So understood, Christian "speculation" (theology?) is "quite in order" since it "speculate[s] within a presupposition" (p. 377).

might then be developed.[13] And when writing in his own *Journals and Papers*, Kierkegaard can say, "It [reason] believes the paradox, and now ... reason is properly determined to honor faith, specifically by becoming absorbed in the negative qualifications of the paradox."[14]

REASON AND CHRISTIAN PHILOSOPHY AND THEOLOGY

I conclude this short survey by noting that human reason is an important part of Christian philosophy and theology for Paul, Luther and Kierkegaard alike (although in very different ways in the details of their thought). Philosophy can proceed in a way that is deeply faithful and Christian, and Christian theology has always aspired to nothing more than this. Of course the presuppositions, practices and value commitments that make philosophical reasoning possible in the first place will not for the whole community of philosophers today be a *Christian* faith; but will it not be something we might rightly call a faith of some kind? Does not each philosopher, too, come with perspectives, fundamental trusts, emotions, embodiment and human flesh? Not that these would be the same for all philosophers: perish the thought! However, philosophy as a tradition of inquiry and intellectual conversation always and everywhere involves such things, sometimes at a deep level. "Faith" is found in both philosophy and theology, in both the right use of human reason and true religion.

CONCLUDING UNSCIENTIFIC REMARKS

More points in dialogue with this engaging chapter could be made. I would have wished to point out in detail that the treatment of analytic philosophy is a dated and a caricature, or to speak in praise of the many fine elements of CRC, but there is no space. My main point in positive terms is this: as Christian philosophers and theologians we should accept the biblical and theological truths about reason, both sinful reason and redeemed reason. For Christ wants to be Lord of body, mind and heart for both the individual *and* the community, a Master who is at once also

---

[13]Kierkegaard, *Concluding Unscientific Postscript*, 1:377.
[14]*Kierkegaard's Journal and Papers*, trans. H. V. Hong and E. Hong (Bloomington: Indiana University Press, 1967), 1:628.

a humble servant. There is a place in the life of Christian faith for the renewal of our minds, too, without pretending that the mind is the most important or godly part of us. Following him means learning to love God with all we are: heart, soul, body and, yes, even our mind. But this means that for Christian faith and faithful reason, the story of conflict will only be a partial truth.[15]

[15]I should like to thank Dr. Sally Bruyneel for some excellent guidance and comments that helped improve this response.

The Synthesis of Reason and Faith Response

Craig A. Boyd

THE FIDEIST APPROACH—or what he calls "faith and philosophy in tension"—that Carl Raschke advocates owes a great deal to the Kierkegaardian tradition that informs much of the existentialist and postmodernist reaction to modernity. That is, by calling into question the modernist notions of "truth" and "reason" we can "make room for faith" by showing that the concepts of truth and reason themselves are part of a larger tradition that already assumes what reason and truth must be even before we can start a discussion. However, Raschke also complicates his argument by selectively appealing to passages of Scripture and the Christian tradition that do not represent a broader Christian consensus about the nature of faith and reason. In fact, Raschke's arguments exclude the majority of the Roman Catholic tradition—as represented in the work of Thomas Aquinas—and much of the Protestant tradition as well—by excluding the Anglicans, Methodists and most of the Pentecostals. Instead of considering the larger Christian tradition he focuses on the epistles of Paul, the Magisterial Reformation and postmodern philosophy. Although I am sympathetic to his attempt at deconstructing some aspects of analytic philosophy—such as the reductionistic tendencies of logical positivism—he fails to consider perspectives that do not fit his Procrustean bed of interpretation.

Alasdair MacIntyre offers a more helpful critique of modern philosophy in his famous work *After Virtue* and demonstrates that our use of important philosophical terms is embedded in a larger narrative.[1] That is, words always have contextual meaning and do not "exist in isolation." On this point, I agree with Raschke but, unfortunately, while he is quick to point out the alleged failings of other "traditions," he fails to consider his own use of "reason" with such rigor. In fact, this equivocation of terms, definitions and meanings combined with straw-man

---

[1]Alasdair MacIntyre, *After Virtue* (Notre Dame: University of Notre Dame Press, 1981).

arguments is the source of a great deal of intellectual confusion. And in some very important respects, the essay is an extended straw-man argument against the "faith and reason" perspective, at times misrepresenting the views of thinkers such as Aquinas and at other times selectively reading the Bible by appealing to Paul above all other authorities.[2]

As I argue in my essay, there are at least three traditions of reason: one associated with the modernist-empiricist tradition, one associated with the Reformed theological tradition and one associated with the tradition of Thomas Aquinas, who held that reason operated in all responsible human activities—including the sphere of faith both prior to and after justification. Raschke conflates the meanings of the logical positivists with that of Aquinas and offers an account of rationality that is thoroughly fideistic in the sense that reason cannot be trusted. After all, Saint Paul didn't trust it, so why should we?

Raschke claims that his own view is "biblical" and that it is the Hebrew idea of "wisdom" that we must adopt. That is, the message of the cross is "foolishness to the Greeks." He says:

> Christ cannot be proven, only *apprehended*. He is apprehended not as human wisdom but as *God's wisdom*, a wisdom that amounts to God taking on the most wretched guise of a crucified criminal in contrast with his infinite majesty in order to overcome once and for all the purely "dialectical" opposition of finite and infinite, human language and the divine, redemptive mystery for all creation. There is no way that reason can reconcile this opposition. (p. 42)

Yet, if we understand reason in the third way that I offer—that is, as the capacity to take into account real relationships and to apprehend truths beyond our own intellect's natural capacity—we see that Raschke's claim falters. In order to "apprehend" Christ we must employ our reason. In order to see the distance between God's wisdom and our own human wisdom we must employ reason. In order to see that a crucified criminal overcomes our sin we must employ reason. In fact, in order to under-

---

[2]A peculiar oddity of the essay is that although it claims to be a "Christian" defense of the Tension thesis, we find that Paul is mentioned or cited forty-seven times, while Christ himself is noted only twenty-eight times. For a Christ follower one would certainly expect Christ to be more prominent.

stand whether reason can or cannot "reconcile" two ideas is to employ reason itself! This is not reason in the fallen and corrupted form of the logical positivists who set out to dismantle theology, but it is the rich tradition of reason found in the work of Augustine, Aquinas, Hooker, Wesley and Lewis.

Raschke continues with his own commentary on the biblical perspective of faith and reason by introducing the work of Derrida, who asks, "Are we . . . *first* Jews or *first* Greeks?" (p. 37). The implicit assumption is that one must have priority. This is how Raschke attempts to gloss over the question Tertullian asked twenty centuries earlier. For Tertullian, Derrida and presumably Raschke himself, we can only identify ourselves in one way with a priority. We are *either* Jews *or* Greeks. We are *either* Christians *or* philosophers. We are *either* disciples *or* dialecticians. One *must* rule over the other. Unfortunately, Raschke never tells us why this is the case. He simply asserts it as an article of faith. (In fact, given his own fideistic proclivities he should probably avoid using all arguments since to employ a form of "reason" would seem to undercut his fundamental commitment to fideism. Rather, he should simply offer a one-word response to the synthesist, "No," which is about all he can say without using the very notion of reason he so vehemently rejects.) What we need to see is an argument delineating why this isn't simply a false dichotomy. Am I the son of my mother or the son of my father? Am I a husband or an American citizen? Is my dog a mammal or does she live indoors? But surely to ask questions of priority here is absurd. Is it possible for one to take one's loyalty to one parent at the expense of the other too far? Yes, but it is absurd to think that this is necessarily the case. But what if philosophy is such a dangerous pursuit that it inevitably tests our loyalties to the faith?

The problematic employment of false dichotomies does not end with whether we are Jews or Greeks. The last section of the essay is titled "Faith Is Not 'Rational' but Relational." The assumption, of course, is that *relationality* and *rationality* are mutually exclusive concepts. The idea of trust that seems central to faith clearly has a relational element to it—in fact it may be primarily relational—as Raschke claims. However, this relationality is also rational. If the logical positivists were the only ones who defined reason as an exercise in propositional logic then Raschke would have scored an important point. However, he neglects the broader tradition of reason. Not only are reason and relationality not mutually exclusive concepts, but they can even mean the same thing if the idea of "ratio" is properly understood. Yet, Raschke fails to note this. At best, Raschke ascribes a narrow and mistaken view of reason to the Christian tradition from Augustine through Aquinas down to C. S. Lewis. At worst, this is a failure to understand the nature of the divine *Logos* John speaks of in the first chapter of his Gospel. Reason or *Ratio* (i.e., the divine *Logos*), unequivocally, is relational—"and lived among us" (Jn 1:14 NRSV). And he was the light who "enlightens" all humanity (Jn 1:9 NRSV).

Early in the essay, Raschke admits that "Tertullian was not reviling philosophy so much as its *misapplication* in the hands of the learned who had lost all sense of what it means to be a Christ-follower first and an intellectual second" (p. 38). Yet, he seems to forget this disclaimer and quickly moves to paint all philosophy with the broad brushstrokes of a misinterpretation of Saint Paul (the passages from 1 Corinthians). Yes, certainly some philosophers were "pretentious windbags" (p. 42)—but so too are many theologians, preachers and other would-be leaders in the church. If we were to take this approach today, we could say the same thing about scientists. The late Carl Sagan, Richard Dawkins and others are nothing more than pretentious windbags who claim to speak the truth about the universe, God and the soul. But if we were to see all scientists in this way we would be condemning an entire group of Christians along with these opponents of the faith. One generation's "philosophers" are merely another's "scientists."

What Raschke assumes is that reason is fundamentally a competitor to faith. It is so dangerous that it must be controlled and subjugated prior to any employment whatsoever. Yet, as we have seen—and as Raschke himself demonstrates so well—there is never any human apprehension or thought that does not employ reason. In order to grasp the truths of the faith one must employ reason as a means to understand oneself as part of the Christian narrative. There is no alternative.

In reference to the work of Thomas Aquinas, Raschke makes the dubious claim that "He adopted Aristotelianism *carte blanche* in order to argue vigorously for the truth of the Christian faith over what he called 'the pagans,' which included both Greeks and Muslims" (p. 47). This is not so. Numerous scholars have demonstrated unequivocally that Aquinas was first and foremost a "Christ follower" and secondly a philosopher. And even then, he often appeals to many other philosophers over and against Aristotle—including Plato. Yet, of all the authorities employed in Aquinas's *Summa Theologiae*, the Scriptures are quoted more than any other source.

Although this is a common mistake, it is also what serves to further complicate matters. Some have used it as the basis for the claim that Christians have "followed" Aquinas down the road to a kind of autonomous rationalism that makes the claims of faith peripheral. Raschke says:

> In both obvious and not so obvious ways Christian philosophy, at least from the mid-twentieth century onward, has taken Aquinas to another level by buying into the covert assumptions of the new science and arguing for the Christian faith as if it were an equal or superior type of scientific rationality with its own kind of internal logic. (p. 48)

If it were true that Aquinas adopted a kind of naive idol worship of Aristotle—and it is not—and if it were true that Christians in the twentieth century followed the lead of "the new science"—and it is not—then Raschke might have a plausible argument. Yet, he does not.

Raschke's proposed solution to the pitfalls of "rationalism" appeals to the allure of postmodernism. He seems to think that this will not be popular among many Christians as there is a presumption against it based upon the mistaken idea that it is relativistic. He claims, "Postmodernism as a philosophical movement historically *has nothing to do with relativism*" (p. 58, emphasis in the original) and "the philosophical language and stances of certified 'postmodern' philosophers themselves cannot by any stretch of the imagination be termed 'relativistic'" (p. 58).[3] He offers a rather convoluted argument by suggesting that they don't know the meaning of the term *relativism*.

---

[3]For a concise refutation of Raschke's claim about postmodernism not being relativistic, see my *A Shared Morality: A Narrative Defense of Natural Law Ethics* (Grand Rapids: Brazos Press, 2007), especially chapter 5. Although I argue against "moral relativism" (i.e., the idea that moral values have no ultimate basis in a transcendent reality) it can also be used against epistemic relativism.

The mistake here is threefold: (1) Raschke fails to offer any definition of *relativism* that might be helpful, (2) he fails to consider the most prominent postmodernist thinker of the past fifty years, Richard Rorty, and (3) he fails to see that at least with regard to the main subjectivist thrust of postmodernism that it cannot fail to be relativistic because it is self-referential. The first problem is a failure to define the term. He accuses his interlocutors of "distorting the meaning of technical terms" (p. 58) without offering a definition himself. Relativism could be moral relativism, cultural relativism or epistemological relativism. We glean from his later comments that he seems to mean epistemological relativism. This type of relativism is one that denies that we can know with any kind of certainty the "world out there."

The second mistake is a "sin of omission," as Raschke simply fails to consider Rorty as one of the "certified" postmodern philosophers. (Who gives the "certification" in these instances? Raschke himself?) If we allow for the fact that most (with the exception of Raschke) see Rorty as one of the most influential postmodern philosophers, we must take his work seriously. And Rorty readily admits that his views are epistemologically relativistic.

> We need to make a distinction between the claim that the world is out there and the claim that truth is out there. To say that the world is out there, that it is not our creation, is to say with common sense that things in space and time are the effects of causes that do not include human mental states. To say that truth is not out there is simply to say that where there are no sentences there is no truth, that sentences are elements of human language, and that human languages are human creations.[4]

"Truth" really has no meaning apart from a convenience that we have afforded it. Yet, clearly, if we can never escape from the confines of our language—as both Derrida and Rorty admit—how can we ever understand whether our statements are true or not?

The third mistake is the most problematic. The truth is that postmodernism, when employed as Raschke has used it, does indeed lead to a

---

[4]Richard Rorty, *Contingency, Irony and Solidarity* (New York: Cambridge University Press, 1989), p. 5.

kind of epistemic relativism—his objections notwithstanding.

> Deconstruction cannot limit itself or proceed immediately to a neutral-
> ization: it must, by means of a double gesture, a double science, a double
> writing, practice an *overturning* of the classical opposition *and* a general
> *displacement* of the system. . . . Each concept, moreover, belongs to a
> systematic chain, and itself constitutes a system of predicates. There is no
> metaphysical concept in and of itself. There is a work—metaphysical or
> not—on conceptual systems. Deconstruction does not consist in passing
> from one concept to another, but in overturning and displacing a con-
> ceptual order.[5]

The deconstruction Derrida employs attempts to overthrow any and all metanarratives. It is a kind of "unraveling" of a story that was just a myth in the first place. Once we see that the "emperor has no clothes" we are free to reject any claim to metaphysical "truth." But in this radical rejection of "truth" and what it refers to, it follows that no position is tenable—or conversely, that all positions are tenable.

MacIntyre, again, is illuminating at this point. He sees Derrida (and others like Nietzsche and Foucault) as "genealogists." That is, they at-tempt to deconstruct the rationalist enterprise of Kant and the French Enlightenment thinkers by tracing the origins of words and their con-texts. When this is done, one can see that these words have no objective meaning. Rather, terms like *good* and *noble* are self-descriptors, while terms like *evil* and *base* describe others. This is a traditional in-group versus out-group comparison. MacIntyre says,

> What has . . . very rarely, if at all, attracted explicit genealogical scrutiny
> is the extent to which the genealogical stance is dependent for its concepts
> and its modes of argument, for its theses and its style, upon a set of con-
> trasts between it and that which it aspires to overcome—the extent, that
> is, to which it is inherently derivative from and parasitic upon its antago-
> nisms and those towards whom they are directed, drawing its sustenance
> from that which it professes to have discarded.[6]

---

[5]Jacques Derrida, *Margins of Philosophy*, trans. Alan Bass (Chicago: University of Chicago Press, 1982), p. 329.
[6]Alasdair MacIntyre, *Three Rival Versions of Moral Inquiry* (Notre Dame: University of Notre Dame Press, 1991), p. 215.

The genealogist is inescapably caught in the bind of self-referentialism. Any kind of argument she proposes must—on her own grounds—be rejected as it is appealing to some form of epistemological realism (i.e., that we can actually discern the true from the false).

Bernard Williams makes a similar point against Rorty when he says,

> [The genealogy project] is self-defeating. If the story he tells were true, then there would be no perspective from which he could express it in this way. If it is overwhelmingly convenient to say that science describes what is already there, and if there are no deep metaphysical or epistemological issues here but only a question of what is convenient . . . then what everyone should be saying, including Rorty, is that science describes a world already there. But Rorty urges us not to say that, and in doing so, in insisting, as *opposed to* that, on our talking of what it is convenient to say, he is trying to reoccupy the transcendental standpoint outside human speech and activity which is precisely what he wants us to renounce.[7]

We see again here the unfortunate self-referentialism inherent in any form of postmodernism. It is inescapable and provincially self-limiting. A more robust approach has to assign at least a minimal role to human reason. Otherwise we consign ourselves to a solipsistic fideism that has no engagement with the world "out there."

---

[7]Bernard Williams, *Ethics and the Limits of Philosophy* (Cambridge, MA: Harvard University Press, 1985), pp. 137-38.

2

Faith Seeking Understanding

Collegiality and Difference in Theology and Philosophy

Alan G. Padgett

Hᴜᴍᴀɴ ᴋɴᴏᴡɪɴɢ ᴇɴɢᴀɢᴇs ʙᴏᴛʜ faith and reason. All human learning draws upon trust, to some degree, and develops with critical reasoning and reflection. In this chapter I will present a view of theology and philosophy in which faith and reason work together in both, but in different ways. This model has roots in the teachings of Scripture and in the writings of some classic Christian thinkers, especially Augustine and Anselm. Among evangelicals it can be found in John Calvin as well as John Wesley and Jonathan Edwards and has many followers past and present.[1] Borrowing from Anselm, we can call this model "faith seeking understanding."[2]

To start with, we will see that the differences between faith and reason do not match up precisely with the differences between theology and philosophy as academic disciplines. We will then look at the ways in which Christian faith is or is not essential to the communal and traditional enterprise of philosophy and theology. I will propose that theology and philosophy are best understood as different academic disciplines or traditions of inquiry, which can at certain points work together as col-

---

[1]I use the word *evangelical* in a broad theological sense to refer to a theology rooted in the gospel of Jesus Christ. See further Donald Bloesch, *A Theology of Word and Spirit* (Downers Grove, IL: InterVarsity Press, 1992), pp. 20-24.

[2]Anselm, *Proslogion*, in *The Major Works*, ed. Brian Davies and G. R. Evans (New York: Oxford University Press, 1998), p. 87. Anselm is indebted to Augustine on this point, as he often is. See, e.g., Augustine, *De Fide et Symbolo* ("A Treatise on Faith and the Creed"), in *Nicene and Post-Nicene Fathers*, series 1, ed. P. Schaff (1887; Grand Rapids: Eerdmans, 1978), 3:231 (cited henceforth as NPNF 3).

leagues in the development of a Christian worldview. Like colleagues in
a workplace, they may agree or disagree, conflict or mutually support;
what I reject is the idea that one will always set the stage for the other in
interdisciplinary work.

Faith seeking understanding, as a model for theology and philosophy
(or any science, really), has two dynamic movements. The first is a foundation in Christian, biblical faith, which then leads to a discipleship of
the mind, seeking greater wisdom and understanding of God, ourselves
and creation. In this way the model of faith seeking understanding is
different from views that move *from* human understanding of the world
to faith in God (e.g., classical Thomism or natural theology). The second
movement in the model I will defend here is a kind of reflection upon
and reasoning about our theology and practice from the perspective of
critical, philosophical or scientific reason. Here both "secular" and "redeemed" reason can be very helpful in raising questions, pointing out
serious problems and proposing new avenues of thought. Christian faith
and right reason move in a dynamic interplay, drawing upon several
disciplines, with the goal of wisdom, understanding and knowledge—all
part of our general discipleship in Christ, the Wisdom of God. Both
movements are biblical and traditional, but they are not always put together in just this way. As an extended example of what I am talking
about, we will look at how Christian theology is in dialogue with philosophy, and vice versa, concerning the doctrine of the Trinity.

As part of explaining this dynamic model of Christian wisdom, in
which both theology and philosophy play important roles, we will discover that human reason is never purely value neutral. Even when seeking
to be objective in the best sense, human reasoning is a value-laden enterprise. Because this is so, our reasoning can be corrupted by sin and evil.
For this reason, it is important for Christian wisdom that reason can be
redeemed, that is, grounded on faith in Christ and illuminated by the
Holy Spirit. Therefore we ought to affirm as Christian believers that a
robust trust in the Lord is lived out (in part) by a quest for truth, understanding and knowledge. Both the Bible and much of the Christian tradition value reason and are critical of the pretensions of the human heart
and mind. So faithful Christians should not fear reason and hard thinking,

while at the same time human thinking needs the purification of the Living Word and the Spirit of God, if we are to achieve the goal of worshiping God with our whole being: heart, soul, mind and strength.

Of course faith, too, can be misplaced. We can trust in the wrong people or put our faith in the wrong teachers or teachings. We can misunderstand Scripture and improperly live out our Christian faith. While some Christians do not appreciate the role of reason for the Christian life today, I will argue on biblical grounds that right reason, grounded in Scripture and Christian faith, plays an essential role in critical reflection upon Christian faith and life for individuals and communities of faith. Thus we will discover that both faith and reason are, in differing ways, essential to full discipleship and mature Christian wisdom—to life in Christ. Theology, philosophy and the sciences are all essential in the development of a mature Christian worldview for the people of God today.[3]

WHAT IS FAITH? TRUST AND HUMAN LEARNING

We begin by calling into question a common duality of faith and reason, which suggests they have nothing to do with each other, or that one is just for religion (faith) while the other (reason) is what science and philosophy are all about. Faith is certainly called for in biblical Christianity, and this faith has many dimensions.[4] While faith in a broad sense includes elements of what is believed in (the content of faith) as well as elements of practice (embodied faith), for now we will focus on faith as a kind of *trust*. It turns out that trust is basic to human learning and thus a part of both philosophy and theology as academic practices or traditions of inquiry.

---

[3]Much of the perspective presented in this chapter I have worked out in detail in previous publications, especially Alan G. Padgett, *Science and the Study of God: A Mutuality Model for Theology and Science* (Grand Rapids: Eerdmans, 2003); "Theologia Naturalis," *Faith and Philosophy* 21 (2004): 493-502; "The Relationship Between Theology and Philosophy," in *For Faith and Clarity*, ed. James Beilby (Grand Rapids: Baker Academic, 2006); and "The Trinity in Theology and Philosophy," in *Philosophical and Theological Essays on the Trinity*, ed. Thomas McCall and Michael Rea (New York: Oxford University Press, 2009), pp. 329-35.

[4]See, among many others, Otto Michel, "Faith," in *New International Dictionary of New Testament Theology*, ed. Colin Brown (Grand Rapids: Zondervan, 1975–1980), 1:587-606; Walter Brueggemann, *Theology of the Old Testament: Testimony, Dispute, Advocacy* (Minneapolis: Fortress, 1997), pp. 466-70.

Developmental psychologists such as Erik Erikson have argued convincingly that basic trust in parents and in the world is a healthy part of human personal development.[5] It is trust rather than doubt that is truly fundamental, although as we mature all of us learn to doubt the world, other people or even ourselves. Yet living in doubt all the time leads to profound anxiety. Thus faith is fundamental to mature human growth, even as reasonable doubt is part of a mature wisdom about the world.

Not only is basic trust part of what it means to be a whole and healthy human being, philosophers such as Michael Polanyi have pointed to the important role that trust plays in human learning in general. In speaking of a "fiduciary programme" at the heart of scientific knowledge (and, by extension, knowing in general), the Hungarian scientist-philosopher wrote: "We must now recognize belief once more as the source of all knowledge."[6] His basic point is that learning is a whole-body experience that involves both embodied practices and "tacit," nonpropositional awareness, which provide the scientist (or any human learner) with a framework in which new discoveries can be made or old theories tested. Without a basic commitment to the presuppositions, practices and tools of a science, developments in that discipline become impossible.[7] To take one famous example, if Galileo did not trust in his eyes and his telescope, he never would have discovered the moons of Jupiter. Likewise, without trust in the tools of logic, analytic philosophy would never have developed. The body and the "heart" (affections, attitudes) are fully involved in human learning. The widely influential education theorist Benjamin Bloom and his colleagues rightly included mind (cognitive), heart (affective) and body (physiomotor) in their holistic "taxonomy" of human learning.[8] Without the so-called heart-dimension of faith, indeed the affective domain in general, there is no proper reasoning for

---

[5]Erik Erikson, *Identity and the Life Cycle* (New York: Norton, 1980), pp. 57-67.

[6]Michael Polanyi, *Personal Knowledge* (Chicago: University of Chicago Press, 1962), p. 266.

[7]See further ibid., pp. 15-18, 59-61, 95-100.

[8]Benjamin S. Bloom, *Taxonomy of Educational Objectives: The Classification of Educational Goals* (New York: Longmans, Green, 1956). See also Jean Piaget and Bärbel Inhelder, *The Psychology of the Child* (New York: Basic Books, 1969) for an integrated model of development and mental function. These earlier works need to be supplemented by developments in neuroscience, e.g., Louis Cozolino, *The Neuroscience of Human Relationships: Attachment and the Developing Brain* (New York: Norton, 2006).

humans. We can have an uncritical, immature trust without critical reason; but there is no reasoning without faith.

WHAT IS REASON?

When we talk about faith and reason it is easy to think of these as special, distinct properties that are pieces of us. But our quick look at basic trust shows us that trust and thinking are not separate parts of the human mind or particular organs of sense, but simply the whole human being properly functioning. Trusting and thinking are distinguishable *activities of the whole person*, and a whole human person includes the body. Scientists have recently argued (rightly, to my mind) that human reason always includes an element of feelings (affective learning) and, further, that the human brain functions properly only in the larger context of the neural network and the whole body—including connections with others.[9] Yet much of Christian thinking was formed by an outmoded psychology, in which feeling and thinking were wrongly associated with certain organs (brain, heart) or certain parts of the soul (faculties or senses like mind and will), while the soul was viewed as a different thing from the body. A more holistic understanding of human thinking, which sees learning as a whole-body function, also helps us to overcome the false dichotomy between faith and reason. Of course, learning is not only dependent upon trust. Human thinking is grounded in our embodied existence in the world. We can distinguish, but should never separate, the various elements of mental function and rational development.

Like other aspects of human existence, reason is a gift of God. The Bible values human reason and wisdom. "The fear of the Lord is the beginning of wisdom; fools despise insight and learning" (Prov 1:7, my translation). While some Christian groups are highly suspicious of human reason, the Bible sees learning, reason and wisdom as gifts to be used for God's glory. Thinking is natural to humanity, a normal part of our created abilities. This is why the greatest commandment, according to Jesus, involves the life of the mind: it is part of the whole person who loves and follows after God. "Love the Lord your God with all your heart,

---

[9]See, among many works, Antonio Damasio, *Descartes' Error: Emotion, Reason, and the Human Brain* (New York: Putnam, 1994); Cozolino, *Neuroscience*.

and with all your soul, and with all your strength, and with all your mind" (Lk 10:27 NRSV; see also Deut 6:5). Biblical religion does not have a problem with thinking, learning or human knowledge. It *does* have a problem with human thinking when it sets itself against the purposes of God. When human reason becomes idolatrous, when it is distorted and used for evil, it becomes a serious problem for both the biblical authors and for Christians today. When we begin to see that reason is a function of the whole embodied human person, we also begin to understand the limits of human reason and the possibilities for its corruption.

While the Scriptures value reason and wisdom, they do not always speak of human reason in positive terms. For example, in Colossians Paul warns the church, "See to it that no one takes you captive through philosophy and empty deceit, according to human tradition" (Col 2:8 NRSV). But warnings like these need to be seen in their larger context to be properly understood. Paul was one of the first great intellectuals of the church. He valued wisdom, understanding and knowledge. But he grounded the quest for truth in Christ. This becomes clear if we take the time to read the all of Colossians 2. He begins the chapter by telling the church that he wants them to be "encouraged and united in love." Why? "So that they may have all the riches of assured understanding and have the knowledge of God's mystery, that is, Christ himself, in whom are hidden all the treasures of wisdom and knowledge" (Col 2:2-3 NRSV). The problem they were having in Colossae was that some believers were being led astray by heretical, non-Christian teachings.[10] This is what Paul is objecting to: not the love of wisdom itself, but any human reasoning that sets itself up against the lordship of Christ (Col 2:6-8). The lesson we learn should be this: knowledge is good, but can be corrupted by sin. Wisdom is a good thing, and so is the love of wisdom (*philosophia*); but loving the Lord our God with all our mind is greater still. This is why Paul elsewhere urges us to "take every thought captive to the obedience of Christ" (2 Cor 10:5, my translation).[11]

---

[10]For more on this letter and its background, see Robert McL. Wilson, *A Critical and Exegetical Commentary on Colossians and Philemon*, International Critical Commentary (London: T & T Clark, 2005), pp. 1-63.

[11]For the sake of convenience, I speak of Paul as the author of both letters, although this is sometimes disputed by biblical scholars.

Reason is a gift of God, but it is not the highest aspect of our existence. Common in early Christian writers like Augustine was the view that reason is the "highest" human function, that part of the soul (and they did divide the soul into parts) which is the most divine, the "image of God" in us.[12] This view has more to do with Plato than with Scripture. When the Bible speaks of our being created in the image of God, it never mentions reason or the mind.[13] Even though Augustine's view had more to do with Platonism than Scripture, it seems, his view of reason as the highest of the soul's functions has been highly influential. Be that as it may, it must be resisted, and for good reasons. Scripture and modern sciences both teach us differently: reason is important but not the most important part of being human. It is our whole being that is made in the image of God, and mental function is not the most important part of this.

Does reason need redemption? Using their God-given powers of thinking, human beings are able to learn and become wise, to think and to grow in knowledge and understanding of themselves, of God and of the world around them. Yet like everything human, thinking has its limits and inherent dangers as well as its joys and triumphs. The study of the nature, possibility and limits of knowledge is the task of epistemology, one of the central elements of philosophy. Like other areas of philosophy, epistemology is fascinating and very complex. We can hardly take up the tasks and questions of epistemology adequately in this short section. Still, in laying out the differences between theology and philosophy we will take a brief detour into the philosophy of science, touching on a few issues in epistemology. Before we turn to theology and philosophy as academic disciplines, though, we should end this section by speaking of the value of human reason for religious faith.

Just as trust and thinking always work together in healthy human development and learning, so also academic reason and religious faith ought to work together. Our goal should be a holistic human wisdom, which is fully scientific and philosophically sound, and also fully spir-

---

[12]For example, see Augustine, *The Trinity* 14.4, in NPNF 3:186-87.

[13]See Genesis 1:26-28; 9:6; 1 Corinthians 11:7. Compare Mark 12:16-17 (Matthew 22:20-21), where the Greek text has "image" (*eikōn*), that is, both Caesar's image (the face on the coin) and God's image (the human person). See also Psalm 8.

itual, religious and ethical. Such a holistic wisdom is part of what it means to follow Jesus as Savior and Lord and the goal of the discipleship of the mind. The Bible consistently speaks of a wisdom that is godly and oriented to the worship of the LORD and an obedient life in the reign and realm of God. We have already seen that this is true in Proverbs, the Gospels and Colossians, and references to Scripture could be multiplied (e.g., 1 Cor 1:18–2:16). It is not so much knowledge per se that the Bible commends but God-centered wisdom, and knowing God in particular. Even when we put the point in these terms—discipleship of the mind, godly wisdom, knowing the Lord—it is clear that human thinking and reasoning is bound to be an essential activity. It may be reason illumined by Christ and grounded in Christian faith, but it will nevertheless be human reasoning. The Holy Spirit will "guide you into all truth" (Jn 16:13 KJV), and this implies that the use of our rational powers, guided by faith and the Spirit, is important for Christian life in general. In theology this is especially so. A mature biblical faith will seek greater understanding, seek the truth where it can be found and not run from reasoning about the faith out of fear that somehow God will not be honored.

Reasoning about faith? But now a critical question raises its head concerning the difference between *Christian* faith and critical reasoning. Faith in God is not like other areas of trust, since it is ultimate. Our whole lives rest upon our highest allegiance, our deepest and profoundest trust, our worship of God and God alone, and our obedience to him in all things. How can human reason have anything to do with this deepest of commitments? Does not this deepest faith require a "leap" that goes beyond proof? The answer to questions like these is not all that difficult, as long as we don't make a classic mistake. The problem here for a critical, self-reflective Christianity might be put in terms of the distance required for rational criticism and evaluation. Maybe we could put it this way: critical reason (as used in philosophy and the sciences) treats a matter of ultimate faith as a mere hypothesis. This kind of rational distance implies an openness to question and doubt, which raises a serious problem for some theologians and philosophers of religion. They would argue that rational criticism of the faith treats the deliberations of faith as hypothetical, and is thus contrary to faith. This viewpoint can be traced back through the twentieth century to the great Christian philosopher Søren Kierkegaard.[14] Even though the work of Kierkegaard is significant and often quite deep, on this point his pseudonym (Climacus) overstates the case.[15] There are different moments and models in the life of faith itself. Critical reflection upon the fact that we find ourselves believing in something (or Someone) *is a normal part of the life of faith*, once we enter into it. Our deepest, ultimate faith may go beyond reason—it may be deeply existential—but even our deepest existential commitments can be brought to light and subjected to rational exploration. (I do not say *proof*, please note, but simply *exploration* by the mind.) Critical reflection is not perfectly objective in any case, and so it need not mean the believer loses her "essential subjectivity" and "infinite personal passionate interest," which Climacus (Kierkegaard) insists is essential to true Christian faith.[16]

The discipleship of the mind in following Christ is open to reasonable criticism. Christian faith should not seek to isolate itself from dialogue and discussion with the larger culture, including the learning of the day, whether philosophical or otherwise. The Christian philosopher Basil Mitchell, among others, defends this point well.[17] He argues convincingly that criticism, the reasoned examination of argument and evidence, is itself based upon some kind of trust or faith, which is part of every worldview. Mitchell goes on to insist that *faith also demands criticism*. Faith in God as creator and redeemer in history, and as the ultimate reality and truth, leads us in our reflective moments to wonder what public evidence we might give for our Christian faith, or at least some parts of it. How might we reasonably reply to critics of Christianity? This bal-

---

[14]Another example would be D. Z. Phillips, following some of Wittgenstein's ideas (see Phillips, *The Concept of Prayer* [New York: Shocken, 1967], p. 14). Through his Viennese education Wittgenstein himself was influenced by both Kierkegaard and Kant.

[15]See, e.g., "The Speculative Viewpoint," in *Kierkegaard's Concluding Unscientific Postscript*, trans. David F. Swenson (Princeton, NJ: Princeton University Press, 1941), pp. 49-55, which Kierkegaard wrote under a pseudonym. Kierkegaard is not the only one with this kind of problem. An opposite error is made by rationalists like G. E. Lessing in his 1777 tract *On the Proof of the Spirit and of Power* (which created his famous "ugly ditch" between faith and history). Lessing assumes that religious truths are somehow "necessary truths of reason." On the contrary, religious truths are almost never logically necessary propositions ("truths of reason"). See Henry Chadwick, ed., *Lessing's Theological Writings* (Stanford: Stanford University Press, 1957), p. 53.

[16]Kierkegaard, *Concluding Unscientific Postscript*, pp. 51, 53.

[17]Basil Mitchell, *Faith and Criticism* (New York: Oxford University Press, 1994).

anced view of faith and critical reason can be found in other thinkers from other times, but Mitchell is one clear representative of this position. The point is not some kind of final proof beyond doubt. It is more a matter of what Stephen T. Davis has called "soft apologetics," that is, explaining the reasonableness of Christianity by starting with faith.[18]

I have been arguing against what we might call "fideism," the view that religious faith does not need critical reason to understand itself and to grow. In a similar vein, we must defend the idea of a rational exploration of faith against certain tendencies among some followers of the highly influential philosopher Ludwig Wittgenstein.[19] The problem with the Wittgensteinian approach to the relationship of faith and reason is the way it treats the "grammar" of faith. Wittgenstein once remarked, "In religious discourse we use such expressions as: 'I believe that so and so will happen,' and use them differently to the way in which we use them in science."[20] For example, Wittgenstein would reject reading biblical language about the incarnation of the Son of God in a factual way as Christians traditionally do, as a hypothesis. Belief in the incarnation, he would argue, is a "grammatical remark" about living in, and making sense of, a deeply Christian way of life. It is not (for the Wittgensteinian) a factual statement, but language that describes a form of life, a Christian way of being in the world, which makes sense only as part of that whole picture. Wittgenstein objected to Christian philosophers who attempt to demonstrate the reasonableness of Christian faith. "Not only is it [Christian faith] not reasonable," he wrote, "but it doesn't pretend to be. What seems to me ludicrous about O'Hara [a Catholic philosopher] is his making it appear to be *reasonable*."[21]

---

[18]See Stephen T. Davis, *Risen Indeed: Making Sense of the Resurrection* (Grand Rapids: Eerdmans, 1993). A similar position is advanced by William Placher in *Unapologetic Theology: A Christian Voice in a Pluralistic Conversation* (Louisville, KY: Westminster John Knox Press, 1989), a deeply philosophical volume from a theologian.

[19]For two brief introductions to Wittgenstein and religion, see John Hyman, "Wittgensteinianism," in *A Companion to Philosophy of Religion*, ed. P. Quinn and C. Taliaferro (Oxford: Blackwell, 1997), pp. 150-58; and Garth Moore with Brian Davies, "Wittgenstein and the Philosophy of Religion," in *Philosophy of Religion: A Guide to the Subject*, ed. Brian Davies (Washington, DC: Georgetown University Press, 1998), pp. 27-33.

[20]Ludwig Wittgenstein, *Lectures and Conversations on Aesthetics, Psychology, and Religious Belief*, ed. Cyril Barrett (Berkeley: University of California Press, 1966), p. 57.

[21]Ibid., p. 58. His italics.

Teasing out the meaning of Wittgenstein's cryptic remarks concerning religion would take us too far afield, and his views can be interpreted in more than one way.[22] While he rightly points to religious practice and life as the space within which religious language makes sense, he seems (if I understand him correctly) to omit the idea that faith itself might demand some kind of critical examination, rational exploration and defense against criticism. What is more, establishing the *meaning* of religious language, where his approach has its strength, does not establish the *truth* of what religious language claims. As such, a mature intellectual faith might engage factual issues drawn from other areas, including from the sciences or philosophy, without losing its vital connection to spiritual life. Sure, the meaning of religious language is found within the community of speakers, within a religious life and practice. At the same time—and this is crucial—exploring the *truth* of religious language may include issues and criteria outside the "language-game" of religion. Thus a pluralistic academic discipline such as history or philosophy can and should raise critical questions about the *truth* of Christian claims, even when the *meaning* of those claims is deeply embedded in an entire way of life.

Finally, to balance out our discussion, we ought to say a word about rationalism. The Enlightenment tended to lean on human reason and the sciences too strongly, asking them to do more than was in fact reasonable. Science and Reason (with capitals, of course) were looked to as some kind of new light for all areas of society, including as a basis "natural" religion. This move turned out to be a dead end in Western thought.

To set human reasoning on too high a pedestal is to do it a disservice. Our minds are complex and quite powerful, but we are mortal beings of clay, and human reason is limited and often goes astray. The postmodern turn in philosophy, from Kierkegaard and Nietzsche to our own day, has rightly criticized the rationalist pretensions of the Enlightenment. Science is indeed wonderful, but when we try to turn science and technology into a pseudo-religion or comprehensive worldview, the end

---

[22]A useful beginning in this regard is James Kellenberger, *The Cognitivity of Religion: Three Perspectives* (Berkeley: University of California Press, 1985), which includes a balanced discussion of "Neo-Wittgensteinian" philosophers of religion such as D. Z. Phillips.

result is a truncated understanding of ourselves and the world. If we insist that what humans can know is limited to the so-called scientific method, we place too much of a burden on these particular disciplines. Both philosophy and theology provide us with knowledge that goes beyond, but should not ignore, the solid discoveries of science. Rationalism and scientism are quite out of fashion these days, at least among philosophers and theologians. We don't need to spend too much time beating what ought to be a dead horse.[23]

THEOLOGY AND PHILOSOPHY: DIFFERENCE AND COLLEGIALITY

So far in this chapter I have been arguing that trust and thinking belong together for human learning and development of all kinds. By extension, therefore, religious faith and critical thinking also belong together. I have argued against fideism, that Christian faith in the God of truth and of creation should be open to critical self-examination and happy to be helped by other disciplines, including philosophy, history or the sciences. I have also briefly rejected the rationalism found in some forms of Enlightenment thought and the scientism still found in our contested cultural space today. We need to avoid both extremes, both kinds of error. Our goal as a believing community that is truth-seeking and worshipful is a religious and scientific worldview that is intellectually satisfactory and biblically sound. This is of course a *project*, not an achievement, for any believer or any church.

To speak of the relationship between philosophy and theology would seem to call up a definition of them both—but none in the strict sense is forthcoming. There are no accepted definitions of these two disciplines. There are some generally accepted things we can say about them, however, before I go on to hazard a working definition for our present purposes.

First of all, while theology and philosophy are both rigorous academic disciplines, they also speak to that which is beyond academics. Theology

---

[23]For more on the postmodern turn in philosophy, see Alan G. Padgett and Steve Wilkens, *Christianity and Western Thought*, vol. 3, *Journey to Postmodernity in the Twentieth Century* (Downers Grove, IL: IVP Academic, 2009). On "scientism" and its problems, see Mikael Stenmark, *Scientism: Science, Ethics, and Religion* (Aldershot: Ashgate, 2001); see also Alvin Plantinga, *Where the Conflict Really Lies: Science, Religion, and Naturalism* (New York: Oxford University Press, 2012).

in this chapter means Christian doctrine, what is sometimes called dogmatics or systematic theology. The origin of Christian teaching is found in faith in and worship of Jesus Christ and, therefore, also of the triune God. When Christians worship together, their hymns, prayers, liturgies and sermons already contain a good deal of Christian doctrine. Theology is not made up in the seminary or university, but already found in the Christian way of life. Here Wittgenstein was surely right. Christian doctrine is caught up in Christian practice, that is, in the Christian way of being in the world, both for individual believers and also for a community of the Spirit.

When we speak of the relationship between theology and philosophy, however, we will need to focus on theology as an equally rational, academic discipline. Christian doctrine is a discipline that studies God and other things in their relationship to God. It seeks the truth about God and the world based upon revelation from God, which finds its center in Jesus the Messiah: the way, the truth and the life (Jn 14:6). Other religions will thus have different theologies (or religious philosophies) based upon their differing understandings and starting points.

Philosophy, too, as the "love of wisdom," points to that which is already larger than the academy. Every person has a basic way of looking at the world, themselves and other people that informs their day-to-day activities. We could call this a philosophy of life or a worldview. A worldview is, broadly speaking, our understanding of who we are, and the world in which we live, including our system of values and our religious beliefs (if any).[24] I use "worldview" in a broad and flexible way and allow that various communities of faith will develop differing worldviews. Indeed, people within the same broad worldview will have important differences among them. The point is that any functioning adult human operates with some philosophy of life or worldview, however implicit. One task of philosophy is to make our worldviews clear and to criticize them based upon reason and experience.

This can be done well by people outside of the academy. Philosophers are not limited to colleges and universities! Still, for the most part, in this

---

[24]For more on worldviews, see Padgett, *Science*, pp. 74-77; see further David Naugle, *Worldview: The History of a Concept* (Grand Rapids: Eerdmans, 2004).

chapter we will be speaking of philosophy as an academic discipline. As such, philosophy seeks the truth. It does so based upon our common resources as humans, especially reason and experience. Philosophy seeks to answer the larger questions of life.[25] It does not normally concern itself with details about factual matters, which it is happy to leave to the natural and human sciences. Rather, philosophy seeks truth about issues of meaning, interpretation, value, beauty and existence as a whole, but always with an eye to rationality, clarity, evidence and argument. Philosophy thus reflects upon the methods and findings of the other disciplines as examples of human ways of knowing without seeking to establish or refute their results. As a whole community, philosophers do not do their work on the basis of faith in Jesus, but upon common human reason and experience. In this broad sense philosophy is common to all literate human cultures.

Informal reasoning and traditions of inquiry. Still, no one begins life as a philosopher or theologian. We grow and develop over time, learning from others, our environment and our experience. At first we are handed our worldview and our language by our earliest communities in which we first discover ourselves. But as we develop intellectually, we want a better grasp of truth about the world, humanity, our values and the divine. In short, we want to improve our worldview when we can. In science, philosophy and theology, knowledge is very infrequently given through demonstrative, formal reasoning. Much of what goes on outside mathematics and formal logic is based upon *informal* reasoning. Some philosophers, going back to David Hume, have called into question this type of "inductive" or informal reasoning. I cannot here give a full defense of informal reason against the skepticism of Hume and others, since I have proposed a solution elsewhere at length. But I think this topic is so important to the relationship between theology and phi-

---

[25]The Chinese philosopher Fung Yu-Lan defines philosophy "very briefly" as "systematic, reflective thinking about life." He then goes on to describe what he means by systematic and reflective, also noting that "Life is an all-inclusive whole." The activity of philosophy he calls "the inner-directed development of the human mind." *A New Treatise on the Methodology of Metaphysics* (Beijing: Foreign Language Press, 1997), pp. 1-2. Cf. Edward Craig, *Philosophy: A Very Short Introduction* (New York: Oxford University Press, 2002), who writes about "some very general picture of what the world is like," and three basic philosophical questions, dealing with value, reality and knowledge (p. 1).

losophy (not to mention religion and science) that I will summarize that argument here.[26]

We use informal or inductive reasoning all the time, as Hume and other skeptics were well aware. The best reply to Hume's skepticism in his own day was given by Thomas Reid.[27] Reid argued that we stand justified in our commonsense modes of reasoning for everyday life, even if we cannot give an abstract, propositional argument as to why we rely upon them rationally. A universal program of doubt, à la Descartes, is a dead end in epistemology. Moving beyond both Reid and Descartes, in the "dialectical realist" epistemology I find most plausible, there will be a few cases when a *particular* principle comes to be doubted for particular reasons—even when that principle is based upon "common sense." We may not be able to find a justification for our principle of informal thinking, but it is rational to look for one. This open and flexible approach leads to four broad conclusions about informal reasoning. The principles of informal reasoning are, first of all, fallible. We can be wrong about the way we state some principle, perhaps, in holding it at all. Second, some principles may be justifiable on the basis of rational insight (what I call "noetic judgment," because the term *a priori* has been so misunderstood). This would provide further justification beyond common sense or tradition. Third, the principles of informal reasoning within the various academic disciplines are handed on within the tradition of that discipline. What counts as a good argument in law is different from what counts as a good argument in biology, for example, and for good reasons! Within a specific discipline or science, traditional principles of informal reasoning have been successful over a long time and are prima facie justified within that tradition of inquiry. Fourth, there is no simple set of principles that justify all informal reasoning; rather, there are a great many. And they may be different in different contexts. So, finally, I argue that the principles of informal reasoning *must be contextualized within the disciplines*, in order to function there. There may

---

[26]See "Induction after Foundationalism," in Padgett, *Science*, pp. 167-94. For dialectical reason, see chap. 2 of the same work.

[27]See Thomas Reid, *Thomas Reid's Inquiry and Essays*, ed. R. E. Beanblossom and Keith Lehrer (Indianapolis: Hackett, 1983), for a good introduction with key original writings.

be some similarities between "simplicity" (to take one example) in math and biology, but in fact the meaning and use of this criterion is quite different in the two traditions of inquiry. This last point is perhaps the most important one for attending to the *real differences* between Christian theology and philosophy.

It turns out, therefore, that the nineteenth-century dream of a pure logical rationality, a scientific thinking that was value-free and based upon reason and evidence alone, has been overturned. There is no "view from nowhere" for a genuinely human epistemology.[28] While there is thus no perfectly neutral and value-free rationality, the alternative is not the oft-feared relativism of "anything goes." Rather, a modest approach to all "scientific" learning is called for. The results of any disciplined inquiry, including theology, must rationally be open to revision in the light of new questions and new evidence. Of course this includes philosophy, but we need to emphasize that *this kind of epistemological humility applies to academic theology with equal force.* Our theology is not God and is not God's revelation. It is a human good work done by people in response to the Word of God. Theology is not the Word of God itself. So theological conclusions should always be open to reasonable reflection in an academic setting, because theology is an academic discipline.

Any tradition of inquiry (that is, a science or academic discipline) as such seeks rational knowledge. As traditions of inquiry, both theology and philosophy seek the truth. They both pursue good arguments, solid evidence, logical clarity, fairness in debate and sound conclusions. They both are concerned with the larger questions of life. But the focus, goals and methods of these two disciplines are distinct. It is wrong to insist that philosophy or science provides some kind of universal public standard of reasoning and evidence to which Christian theology must be subject. For this reason we should reject the proposals of David Tracy, Schubert Ogden and others, who encourage us to practice theological reasoning on public or universal grounds other than the basic principles of logic. I agree that sound logical reasoning is important for both philosophy and theology. When we are thinking in deductive modes, or using our best informal

---

[28]Thomas Nagel, *The View from Nowhere* (New York: Oxford University Press, 1986).

arguments, we will want to follow sound logical principles and avoid logical fallacies. Let us assume this is true for any rational inquiry, including theology and philosophy. Now if this is all that was meant, well and good. But both Tracy and Ogden are thinking of much more rich and robust accounts of what counts as sound universal reasoning.

Let us focus on Tracy's early work. In *The Analogical Imagination* Tracy states that the terms of theological meaning should be limited to the cultural horizon of our mission, that is, by our broader society, including science. "The theologian," he states, "should argue the case (pro and con) on strictly public grounds that are open to all rational persons."[29] There is a sense in which we should agree here. Theological works should be understandable and clear, so that our various publics may grasp what it is we are saying. If "public" only means open to the public gaze, communicated with clarity in a natural language, then well and good. But if "public" means subject to some supposed public, universal and transdisciplinary standards of what counts as good reasoning and evidence, we should not agree. Only the discipline of logic itself operates like that, and then only for deductive logic. Like other disciplines, Christian theology uses informal and commonsense reasoning in ways that are *contextualized to its unique aim, purpose and tradition.* For *Christian* theology, the ultimate source of truth, meaning and coherence comes from God's special revelation, not from some supposed universal human experience or scientific rationality. The very claim to operate according to universal, transdisciplinary rational principles (beyond deductive logic) is highly dubious. Even deductive, symbolic logic comes in more than one version.

On the other hand, philosophers as a truth-seeking community are not all committed to Christ. While the discipline of Christian theology presupposes Christian faith and values, philosophy as a discipline does not. As a pluralistic community and tradition, philosophy seeks truth in its own way. It appeals to our common humanity and experience, our common ability to think hard about important questions, and our mutual life in the world. Sure, the individual Christian philosopher can and should approach one's own discipline from the broad perspective of

---

[29]David Tracy, *The Analogical Imagination: Christian Theology and the Culture of Pluralism* (New York: Crossroad, 1981), p. 64.

a Christian worldview. Alvin Plantinga has rightly argued that Christian philosophers should begin their philosophical work based upon Christian faith; but philosophy *as a tradition of inquiry* does not.[30] Another way of putting this is to notice that the standards of evidence and reason used by the whole community of philosophers do not *privilege* any religious or nonreligious starting point. Philosophy as a discipline certainly should be open to philosophers who are openly Christian, but it is equally open to Buddhist, Marxist or materialist philosophers as well who reject Christianity. One last point here: we can agree that there are no pure, eternal and essential forms of either philosophy or theology. It is important to note the various philosophical schools, for they will differ in their approach, method and forms of rationality. Philosophy can never encounter a pure and eternal Christian theology, either, for there are varying schools and approaches in the tradition of Christian doctrine as well. Suddenly things are looking complex and *very* interesting.

Christian scholarship. For the most part I will be speaking in this section of academic disciplines, not individual experts. As argued above, the rationality of traditions of inquiry is a learned communal practice and set of values. Becoming a scholar in a particular discipline is like being an apprentice in a guild or union: there are certain assumptions, practices, narratives and values that should be absorbed and mastered, not merely by conceptual learning but also by doing. Like informal reasoning as a whole, the rationality of specific traditions of inquiry is functional, practical, communal and traditional. The differences between and nature of these disciplines or research programs are neither eternal absolutes, nor are they the property of any individual. Such research programs are not all inclusive and make assumptions that call for further philosophical investigation. Thus *traditions of inquiry can be shared by people with differing worldviews.* What they have in common is a real but limited set of shared assumptions, practices, goals and research methods. This is a crucial point for understanding the character of Christian scholarship.

---

[30]The evidence for this is the obvious fact that many perfectly good philosophers are not Christians. We should note that Plantinga's criteria for warranted Christian belief are person-relative. He typically writes about what a Christian can or should or may think, not about what philosophy as a discipline is up to. See his *Warranted Christian Belief* (New York: Oxford University Press, 2000), chap. 11.

Christian scholarship is important to the internal goals of Christian theology. In order to rightly see all things in relationship to God, theologians as a community of scholars need a big picture view of the truth about creatures—all creatures. But theology cannot and will not, on its own, find the truth about these matters. For that we depend upon experts in other fields. Especially important are those experts who are willing to interpret the findings of their discipline for a larger intellectual public. Thus theology relies upon experts in all the academic disciplines who can rightly interpret the results of other arts and sciences. To find the "right" interpretation, Christian theology will look to experts who integrate their Christian worldview with the interpretation of results and conflicts in a particular science or philosophy. For example, Christianity teaches that human beings are created in the image of God. What does this mean for our understanding of human nature today? How does this touch upon psychology, anthropology and sociology? The theologian cannot be an expert in all of these fields. We depend upon others in order to fulfill our vocation.

Fortunately for us, there is a tradition of Christian scholarship that already seeks to understand all of reality from the perspective of a Christian worldview.[31] While each discipline (like philosophy or biology) will maintain its own standards of good reason, evidence and argument, the Christian will approach her academic specialty from a perspective of faith. In other words, the Christian scholar accepts the traditional rationality or paradigm(s) of her specialty, *and strives to be the best philosopher, sociologist or biologist she can be.* But she understands this communal rationality and subject of study in a larger context, the context of her own faith, of Christian scholarship.

This helps in three ways: (1) A Christian worldview funds and founds the metaphysical, epistemological and value commitments of a disciplinary paradigm without imposing itself or prejudicing outcomes of investigation; (2) a Christian worldview provides a broad horizon in which the results of research can be interpreted for the larger culture;

---

[31]For brief introductions to the idea of Christian scholarship, see Arthur Holmes, *All Truth Is God's Truth* (Grand Rapids: Eerdmans, 1977); Holmes, *The Idea of a Christian College* (Grand Rapids: Eerdmans, 1975); Nicholas Wolterstorff, *Reason Within the Bounds of Religion*, 2nd ed. (Grand Rapids: Eerdmans, 1984); and George Marsden, *The Outrageous Idea of Christian Scholarship* (New York: Oxford University Press, 1997).

and (3) when confronted with theories that are currently a matter of intense debate within a discipline, a Christian worldview may sometimes guide the believing scholar in a temporary preference of one theory over another, subject to further review, evidence and argument. The Christian will be guided toward the rival theory or paradigm within a discipline that best fits with her larger worldview, just as any rational being would. This is because we are finally seeking truth, and "fit" with other known truths is an important criterion in informal reasoning. It may be that, in the long run, our worldview will need to change to fit new facts and theories. On the other hand, Christian truth may require that elements of accepted "fact" need to be questioned again. The direction of revision cannot be determined a priori. The basic points I am seeking to make here are two: (1) Christian scholarship can be excellent scholarship and deeply Christian at the same time; and (2) Christian theology is open to learning from the sciences and philosophy but must do its own proper theological work as a distinct rational inquiry.

PHILOSOPHY AND THEOLOGY: CONFLICT AND COLLEGIALITY

So far I have been arguing that the character of informal reasoning and the nature of academic disciplines suggest that while some principles of good reason will be found across the disciplines, each tradition works out its own specific standards of good thinking in the quest for truth. We have resisted the call for "public" theology only if this means some kind of universal reasoning, which typically appeals to natural science as its model. Theology must find its own way of being rational and should not pretend to follow the various methods of the natural sciences. As we have already seen, there may be loose standards of reason that humans share as a whole, and that are shared among the various sciences and academic disciplines. But theologians should firmly resist the siren call of the Enlightenment for some universal, absolute set of criteria that objectively sets the standards of rationality for all people all the time (again, apart from deductive logic). While I certainly am convinced of the basic principles of logic and their application to theological claims, experts in logic nevertheless disagree over some of the basic principles of deduction. Of course Christian theological reasoning should avoid logical fallacies and employ sound logical reasoning. It's just not the case that we can appeal to a robust "scientific thinking" that it must follow.

I have been arguing for one traditional model of collegiality for theology and philosophy, naming this model "faith seeking understanding." I have been talking in the abstract for some time; how about a real-world example? Will theology and philosophy always be in harmony? The quick answer to this question is, "Of course not." Because they are different and appeal to distinct sources of knowledge and wisdom, they can be in conflict. Whether this is a creative tension or an outright contradiction cannot be answered in theory, however. We must look and see.

The Trinity in philosophy and theology. I find the doctrine of the Trinity a good place to look at conceptual connections between philosophy and theology because of the long and complex history of interaction. When it comes to the Trinity, philosophy has been essential and helpful, but it has also challenged traditional theological formulations at times. The range of responses shows that, when it comes to philosophy, there will always be a complex set of contrasting answers to any philosophical question. The Trinity as core Christian doctrine illustrates this diversity.

In the history of the development of the Trinity, philosophy played an early and essential role. While the New Testament has some proto-trinitarian passages, the final form of the doctrine developed later, in conversation with diverse Christian views in the early centuries after the apostles. Theologians were almost as diverse in their opinion as philosophers. No wonder the relationships can be complicated. But we digress. Let's look at a time when philosophical work was essential to the theology of the church.

As the church catholic struggled to express, defend and articulate the doctrines of the Christian faith, philosophical concepts were borrowed from the philosophy and "science" (natural philosophy) of the day.[32] At the Council of Nicaea, for example, the assembled ecumenical leaders

---

[32]For an excellent introduction to the doctrine of the Trinity, see Roger Olson and Christopher Hall, *The Trinity*, Guides to Theology (Grand Rapids: Eerdmans, 2002). For more details about patristic developments concerning the Trinity, including the Council of Nicaea, see Jaroslav Pelikan, *The Christian Tradition*, vol. 1, *The Emergence of the Catholic Tradition, 100–600* (Chicago: University of Chicago Press, 1971), 172-225.

borrowed a term from Greek philosophy to confess a core doctrine of the Trinitarian faith: *ousia* or "being." The Nicene Creed specifically teaches that the Father and the Son are "of the same being" (*homoousion*). With some reluctance the assembly at Nicaea used a nonbiblical philosophical term to express the biblical, Christian faith. Here we have a good example of one way philosophy can be very helpful, even essential, to the task of Christian theology. Without some limited engagement with philosophy, Christian theology is not possible. But theologians must be careful not to be too dependent upon philosophy, not to borrow wholehog an entire system of philosophy.

Since philosophy and theology are in fact *different* in their aims and rationalities, this absorption of philosophy by theology has always resulted in some misunderstanding and distortion. Whether the preferred philosopher is Plato, Kant, Hegel, Whitehead or Derrida (and all these philosophers have been so used by theologians), yielding the central tasks of theology to a single philosopher's work does not have happy results.[33] The church borrowed from philosophy, to be sure, and needs to do so—but only to a limited degree and only when necessary. For example, at Nicaea the church filled the word *ousia* ("being") with its own specific, Christian theological meaning, which became distinct from secular usage precisely because it was God's being that was under discussion. While this borrowing was thus limited, it was real and essential at the time. Philosophy can be very helpful to theology, as long as a proper differentiation is maintained. To borrow some terms from contemporary psychology, the goal of faith seeking understanding is to have a properly self-differentiated relationship with philosophy and human learning in general. Both parties must strive to avoid both total independence and any codependence!

Philosophers have not always been helpful colleagues in the history of Christian theology; they have often been sharply critical. This is just like real colleagues, to be sure, and to be expected. After all, argument

---

[33]For further discussion and defense of this last point, see my chapter, "Putting Reason in Its Place," in Padgett, *Science*. An earlier version of this chapter appeared in a volume dedicated to the discussion of Wesleyan and process theologies, Bryan Stone and Thomas Oord, eds., *Thy Nature and Thy Name Is Love* (Nashville: Kingswood, 2001).

and critique are essential to the philosophical enterprise. And one of the frequent complaints by philosophers over the centuries has been that the doctrine of the Trinity is *incoherent*.[34] Academic theologians have, in differing languages and cultures, worked hard to show that it is coherent, responding to this criticism. This has helped develop and deepen the doctrine. Of course sharp criticism can be helpful, in a way, although not often pleasant. Theologians ignore their critics at their peril, just because theology is a truth-seeking enterprise. Thoughtful and engaged criticism can be a gift. Yet in responding to criticism of the doctrine of the Trinity, some theologians have tended to ignore the need for coherence in Christian theology. They say in effect: "The Trinity is a mystery; what did you expect?" To answer further, we need to look again at the aims and methods that are part of the rationality of theology.

Revelation, mystery and coherence in theology. It is obvious to the casual reader of systematic theology books that no agreed upon methodology, or even a set of schools with differing methods, exists within the broad range of theology today. I am therefore going to limit my remarks to those theologians who believe as I do that Christian theology should be grounded in the gospel of Jesus Christ, and so in the Scriptures and in the great classical tradition of historic Christian faith, as well as the identity-forming practices of the church. For this broad and mainstream approach theologians will look to the Scriptures as the primary sources of revelation. Both Karl Barth and Karl Rahner, theological giants of the twentieth century, sought not only to make the doctrine of the Trinity more meaningful for believers today but also to bring the doctrine more closely into connection with the biblical witness.[35] To take up a contemporary example, it might seem strange that in a book noted for its engagement with analytic philosophy, *Trinity and Truth*, Bruce Marshall does not attend to the work of philosophers on the Trinity.[36] When he discusses the nature and centrality of this doctrine for Christian faith, Marshall draws instead upon Scripture (at least to

---

[34]Among many examples, see Ludwig Feuerbach, "The Contradiction in the Trinity," in *The Essence of Christianity* (New York: Harper, 1957), chap. 24.

[35]Karl Barth, *The Doctrine of the Word of God*, trans. G. W. Bromiley and T. F. Torrance (Edinburgh: T & T Clark, 1956, 1975); Karl Rahner, *The Trinity*, trans. J. Donceel (New York: Crossroad, 1997).

[36]Bruce Marshall, *Trinity and Truth* (New York: Cambridge University Press, 2000).

some degree), classic Christian tradition, including liturgy, and major theologians like Augustine, Aquinas and Luther. I do not find this to be a problem with the book, although it struck me as strange when I first read it. Marshall rightly draws his central notions about the Trinity from the major sources of Christian theological understanding, that is, from Jesus Christ, the Old and New Testaments, and the long ecumenical tradition of consensual and canonical Christian thought, which makes its way into our ecumenical creeds, confessions and forms of worship.

Given this Christ-centered, biblical and evangelical understanding of the goals and sources of Christian doctrine as an academic exercise, it can hardly be thought strange that theologians do not look in the first instance to the work of philosophers on the Trinity. Instead, theologians pay attention to Scripture, the great tradition and the classic theologians of the church in seeking to understand this core doctrine of the faith. In an important work drawing upon both philosophy and theology, *The Divine Trinity*, David Brown follows this approach.[37] It is only after establishing the viability of the doctrine of the Trinity in part two of his book, along with the incarnation, with which it is closely associated, that he then turns in part three to concerns drawn from philosophical issues ("The Coherence of the Doctrine"). This seems to me to be exactly the proper order for Christian theologians in thinking through this complex and essential belief about the biblical God. For it is in consideration of the coherence of the orthodox and biblical doctrine of the Trinity that philosophy can be of the most use to theology. At this point Jerusalem (theology) should work closely with Athens (philosophy) so that both can bring clarity to Christian thought. This ideal is at the root of faith seeking understanding.

Yet we have just noticed a key point at which many philosophers have been highly critical of a key doctrine, insisting that it should be rejected as false and illogical. What happens to the happy idea of collegiality when there is conflict? The charge of incoherence is an important one, which theology should not simply duck. Just like in a working relationship between people, theology owes its colleague (in this case phi-

---

[37]David Brown, *The Divine Trinity* (London: Duckworth, 1985).

losophy) a careful listening and reflection upon their fair criticism. Some response is naturally called for beyond "you just don't understand." Yet when it comes to the doctrine of the Trinity, some theologians have been shy to agree that clarity and coherence are needed. This point about clarity calls for a bit more discussion of what theology is and why coherence is important even with respect to the deep mysteries of faith. To be sure, the search for a coherent theology is not always looked on with favor in today's climate of postmodern sensitivities and religious diversity. May not the whole quest for coherence in theology be a mistake? Is not God beyond human comprehension?

Yes, indeed, God is beyond human understanding. This is the consensual teaching of the ecumenical church. The influential Russian theologian Vladimir Lossky puts it this way: "The dogma of the Trinity is a cross for human ways of thought . . . no philosophical speculation has ever succeeded in rising to the mystery of the Holy Trinity."[38] Certainly the doctrine of the Trinity is a very difficult one to grasp and to teach others. As such it is a cross for human thinking. So if Lossky means that a *complete* explanation of the mystery of the Trinity is impossible through philosophical analysis, then we should agree. That's not going to happen. Theologians often speak of paradox, tension and dialectic, and these are to be expected when we are seeking to speak the truth in human terms of One who is beyond our full understanding. But if Lossky means that philosophy and human reason can bring *no clarity at all* to this mystery, he has gone too far. His statement would then have to be rejected as too apophatic, too much on the negative side of the *via negativa*. In a similar vein on the Roman Catholic side, we can point to the influential nineteenth-century theologian John Henry Newman. In his *Grammar of Assent*, Newman argues that we can find good biblical and traditional reasons to affirm the basic ideas that provide the background for trinitarian orthodoxy. But a clear and logical model of the Trinity is not to be achieved by human reason. "The question is whether a real assent to the mystery, as such, is possible; and I say it is not possible, because, though we can imagine the

---

[38]Vladimir Lossky, *The Mystical Theology of the Eastern Church* (London: J. Clark, 1957), p. 66.

separate propositions [in the dogma of the Trinity], we cannot imagine them together."[39]

In response to views like those of Lossky and Newman, the careful work *of philosophers* on this doctrine shows we must not be too quick to reject coherence in theology. We can indeed "imagine them together," that is, the different elements of the orthodox doctrine, and this is *exactly* the value of philosophical work on the Trinity for the theologian and for the church. For while some philosophers have rejected the doctrine with charges of incoherence, others have worked hard to develop extended models of the doctrine of the Trinity that are coherent and clear.[40] No one should think we can *picture* or imagine the doctrine of the Trinity in any adequate way; but we *can* develop coherent conceptual models.

The task of academic theology as a response to the Word of God is the happy one of seeking to know God from the ground of God's own revelation. As such, theology is a *human good work*. It cannot and should not be confused with revelation itself nor with the being of God. Everything of God is a mystery when rightly understood, for nothing about God can be fully grasped by human thinking or language. And yet God is known in human language, in and among human beings. All theology is about a very deep mystery, therefore, and not just the "difficult" bits. Because theology is a human good work in response to this divine mystery, the language of theology should be as clear, rational and coherent as possible. After all the subject we speak of is complex enough— we should not add to the burden of our listeners with our own obfuscation and incoherence. Dialectic, tension and paradox are not the same as incoherence, because a set of incoherent ideas or statements cannot

---

[39]John Henry Newman, *An Essay in Aid of a Grammar of Assent* (1870; repr., Garden City, NY: Doubleday, 1955), p. 155. Newman goes on to argue that real assent (in his sense) is not possible for the mind, because the imagination cannot image the Trinity. But his general point and attitude toward the mystery of the Trinity is representative of Catholic thought as a whole. See, for example, Aquinas, *Summa theologiae* 1.2.2: trans. Fathers of the English Dominican Province (New York: Benzinger Bros., 1947) "But we cannot know in what God's essence consists, but solely in what it does not consist" (quoting John of Damascus).

[40]For contemporary examples, see the following interdisciplinary collections: Stephen T. David, Daniel Kendall and Gerald O'Collins, eds., *The Trinity: An Interdisciplinary Symposium on the Trinity* (New York: Oxford University Press, 1999); Melville Y. Stewart, ed., *The Trinity: East/ West Dialogue* (Boston: Kluwer Academic, 2003); and more recently the volume by analytic philosophers McCall and Rea, *Philosophical and Theological Essays on the Trinity*.

all be true. As a human good work in response to the grace and Word of God, as faith seeking understanding, theology seeks the truth about God. It therefore must shun incoherence and irrationality. Sometimes "mystery" is evoked as an excuse for sloppy thinking, and this must be anathema to any academic theology worthy of the name. After all, the mystery of God does not end when theology speaks clearly. The simple phrase, "Jesus loves me, this I know, for the Bible tells me so" covers vast, deep mysteries that even the angels gaze into with awe and wonder.

So coherence in theology is no bad thing. Systematic theology seeks to present a coherent wisdom regarding God, humanity and the world, with a special focus on our lives in relationship to God and creatures. Here there is a problem that often arises in interdisciplinary conversations. Important and familiar words do not mean the same thing in different disciplines. So it is with "coherence" in theology and philosophy. For the analytic philosopher coherence is a logical property of propositions in themselves or as a set. Its most basic sense boils down to lack of logical incoherence, that is, an absence of formal inconsistency. While this notion has the merit of being logically precise, it is rarely what theologians mean by "coherence," and many philosophers also mean rather more by the phrase. Often theologians look for things like narrative coherence: the way things fit together and make sense in a story. A classic example of this is in Augustine's *The City of God*. Of course narrative coherence is much vaguer than logical coherence, but the criteria can be useful and meaningful nevertheless.

In addition to this sense of coherence, theologians also look for that broad sense of coherence that idealist philosophers of the early twentieth century, such as F. H. Bradley, named "coherence," that is, the beautiful way that ideas can fit together into a whole. This notion is developed more rigorously by modern followers of coherence theories of justification within epistemology.[41] To take an example from theology, in his classic text *Cur Deus Homo*, Anselm says that he is going to give us "rational and necessary" reasons for why the atonement had to take place. But in the give-and-take of his argument, he very often makes appeal to what is

---

[41]See, e.g., Nicholas Rescher, *The Coherence Theory of Truth* (Oxford: Clarendon, 1973); or Laurence BonJour, *The Structure of Empirical Knowledge* (Cambridge, MA: Harvard University Press, 1985).

"fitting" for God, or due to a moral sense of "right order." These things have more to do with morality and aesthetics than they do with rational necessities.[42] Elsewhere I have called this a "thematic" coherence, and it seems to me the category of rational beauty is the central virtue for theological coherence in this case.[43] We have to say again that theologians do not want their works to be logically incoherent. But the category of "coherence" often means more than logical and conceptual coherence in works of systematic theology. This needs to be remembered by philosophers who read them, and who seek to create coherent models of the doctrine of the Trinity.

There has been a remarkable revival in recent decades of outstanding, highly academic Christian philosophical theology. This has taken place, for the most part, in the tradition of analytic philosophy. Some of these philosophers have spent a great deal of energy, creativity and literary output arguing about the Trinity, while mostly they work with theologians from the distant past or other analytic philosophers.[44] The work of such philosophers, on the other hand, is not very well received by doctrinal or systematic theologians. There are of course notable exceptions to these opening generalizations, but they *are* exceptions to the general rule.[45] For the most part, when theologians today write about the Trinity they often overlook or purposefully dismiss what philosophers are writing on the topic. To embrace the model of faith seeking understanding we have been pressing in this chapter is to see this as mistake. Contemporary theologians *should* pay more attention to what analytic philosophers are up to concerning the Trinity. They ought to welcome the careful, logical and coherent models of the divine Trinity that analytic philosophers have been laboring to construct. Here we can see that once again philosophical work can be a great help to Christian theology.

---

[42]Anselm, *Cur Deus Homo*, preface; 1.1; cf. 1.2.

[43]Alan G. Padgett, "Systematic Theology," in *New Interpreter's Dictionary of the Bible*, ed. K. Sakenfeld et al., 5 vols. (Nashville: Abingdon, 2006–2009).

[44]One recent example of analytic philosophers working on the doctrine of the Trinity is McCall and Rea, *Philosophical and Theological Essays on the Trinity*.

[45]See works already cited: Brown, *Divine Trinity*; Marshall, *Trinity and Truth*; David, Kendall and O'Collins, *The Trinity*; McCall and Rea, *Philosophical and Theological Essays on the Trinity*; see also Thomas McCall, *Which Trinity? Whose Monotheism?: Philosophical and Systematic Theologians on the Metaphysics of Trinitarian Theology* (Grand Rapids: Eerdmans, 2010).

But finally we need to sound another concern. I did mention that the relationships can be complicated, right?

On not leaving it all to Athens. Even when a philosopher is working hard on a particularly difficult issue arising from Christian doctrine, theologians may not embrace their conclusions as readily as the philosopher might wish. This is not so much a conflict as an unwillingness to wholly embrace a particular philosophical position, especially when it is one among other conflicting ones. Once again, I believe theology is wise to maintain some proper boundaries. A particular philosopher may feel that she has finally got it right and solved the conceptual problems of the doctrine in question. She will not be happy when theologians do not agree with her (as they should) and are reluctant to fully embrace her results as the truth about the triune God. It's not that the theologian objects on philosophical grounds to the proposed solution. Rather the theologian simply does not embrace and celebrate this "solution" as such. Is there any way forward beyond this impasse between well-meaning scholars?

Certainly Christian systematic theologians today should be interested in the coherence of the models of the Trinity that philosophers study and (re-)create. But they must not be *too* interested. The work of philosophers on this topic is important *but not central* to the work of Christian doctrine. Thus theologians should pay serious but in some ways limited attention to the work of contemporary philosophers on the Trinity. What I mean by "limited" is just that theology is wise to refrain from fully adopting *one* philosophical model as the right one unless there are solid *theological* reasons for doing so, reasons and evidence that come from the discipline of Christian doctrine.

In the long history of the church and its academic theological reflection, two broad types of thinking about the Trinity have been proposed. The church has never finally adopted one or the other but has worked with both. We can call them the social type and the Latin (or psychological) type. Both of these types find defenders among the great theological doctors of the church as well as contemporary philosophers. On the one hand, the theologian of today should be grateful for the excellent, technical work of analytic philosophers in developing logically coherent and metaphysically plausible versions of the triune God, which follow one or the other of these types (social or Latin). These developed contemporary models, although not compatible among themselves, allow the church to respond well to modern claims that the doctrine of the Trinity is, in and of itself, irrational or incoherent. Yet the importance of this work does not stop here. By developing such careful and sophisticated models the philosopher helps the theologian (and the believer in general) speak with greater precision, clarity and coherence about the triune God. Still, while appreciating this work, the theologian and the church at the same time will not take these models *too* seriously.

It would be wrong in the domain of dogma to take up one specific, elaborate philosophical model to the exclusion of all the others. There just are no theological grounds for such an exclusive claim. In the history of theology, for example, both the social and the Latin type have been followed at different times and by different authors, without any dogmatic exclusions. The church has not selected one and confessed it to be the right view. This would be to take too seriously the ability of philosophers (or theologians) to penetrate into the mystery of the Trinity. Dogmas, remember, are not just true theological statements but decisive confessions of central importance to the identity of the Christian faith. As such, they should be modest affairs, stating what must be stated to maintain the historic, biblical faith in diverse times and places. What is more, the differing models of the Trinity from the patristic age until today sustain important insights and point out serious problems the church would do well to remember. Embracing just one model might steer the faithful too far toward the problems associated with it, ignoring the important correctives that other models provide. The various debates among the philosophical theologians defending different and incompatible (yet fully orthodox) models of the Trinity are worth studying carefully. They add something valuable to the theological conversation and provide a solid reply to skeptical philosophers. But philosophers will not be given the last word on the subject, nor should the church simply adopt one elaborate model instead of the other, within the broad range of orthodox understanding. In general theologians today will be far too respectful of the mystery of God to sign on to any one specific, fully developed philosophical model. Here theologians like Lossky and

Newman provide important cautions we need to take seriously when getting involved in all the technical niceties of philosophical debate.

At this point the serious philosopher might well demure. She has worked hard to develop a sustained model of the Trinity that draws upon significant work in logic, analytic metaphysics and philosophy in general. Having posed the very best viewpoint available, she might well complain that the theologian does not take her work seriously enough to accept it as the true one. While such an attitude is understandable, theology will need to suggest otherwise, and keep up a proper boundary between itself and philosophy. Theology will always take more seriously its sources in special revelation and the Word than even the best-developed philosophical theories based upon them. All such models will have to be taken as provisional and partial, because of the great subject with which we have to deal. It is simply not possible for us to quite so neatly and completely spell out the nature of the infinite Creator whose full comprehension is beyond the ken of mere mortals. This does not mean that orthodoxy is impossible, only that it should always be modest.

CONCLUSION

I have been arguing in this chapter for a model of faith and reason that we have called "faith seeking understanding." Philosophy and theology are both important academic disciplines that can learn a good deal from each other. The work of serious theology is simply not possible without some philosophical engagement with key issues and debates. Theologians can help philosophers by clarifying the teachings and practices of the Christian faith for all who are interested in the Christian faith, and for believing philosophers providing key elements of a larger Christian worldview. Philosophers can assist theologians in their quest for clarity and coherence in seeking to know God and respond properly to the Word of God, both with sharp criticism and with helpful advanced work in philosophical theology. Because all truth is God's truth, philosophers and theologians will want to work closely together as colleagues, without one discipline supplying all the answers or insisting that it sets the framework for future research. By working together, Christian scholars in both theology and philosophy can better follow Christ, the wisdom of God made flesh.

Faith and Philosophy in Tension Response

Carl A. Raschke

ONE OF THE THINGS I FIND MOST unsettling about Alan Padgett's argument is that he seems to confuse "faith" with theology. Indeed, he seems to slide, if not unwittingly then certainly uncritically, between the use of the two words. Even though he seems to be staking out what he would consider an "evangelical" position on the matter, the general argument strikes me as very Catholic in many respects. Catholicism historically, or at least from the High Middle Ages onward, has made a careful distinction between "implicit faith" (*fides implicita*) and "explicit faith" (*fides explicita*).[1] Thomas Aquinas was the first to parse the two terms, which in many respects can be attributed to his realization that in a society administered by clergy people often profess to be Christians without the foggiest notion of what they believe, or why they believe it. Implicit faith for Catholicism traditionally has meant simply assenting to the teachings of the church, which "knows" better than anyone else the true meaning of Christian revelation. Aquinas regarded implicit faith simply as an attitude or disposition. Genuine, or explicit, faith was an "informed" faith, particularly one that had been both reasoned out and conformed to the intellectual consensus of church authorities, living and dead.

During the Reformation of the sixteenth century, however, John Calvin attacked this position as leading to "the most monstrous errors, being received by the ignorant as oracles without any discrimination."[2] Calvin, who believed that faith was impossible without an encounter with God's Word through the reading of Scripture, maintained that it is the illumination of the Holy Spirit—an idea he derived from Augustine—that makes faith real, or "explicit." In other words, Christian doctrine or theological formulations cannot, and do not, constitute the

---

[1]See Thomas Aquinas, *Summa Theologiae* 2.2.2.
[2]John Calvin, *Institutes of the Christian Religion*, trans. Henry Beveridge, Google Mobile Edition (Edinburgh: T & T Clark, 1863), 3.4.2.

foundation of faith. Faith is, as Kierkegaard would later put it over and over and over, an "existential" commitment to following Christ that precedes all theological arguments or convictions. With this commitment both Scripture and Christian doctrine begin to make "sense," insofar as they are cognitive markers of how one as a Christian, therefore, begins to structure and navigate his or her personal life. Once the mind is illumined, everything else slowly begins to fall into place, and one now lives for God, no longer serving the passions of the flesh, as Paul emphasized repeatedly.

Padgett understands faith as a "discipleship of the mind" that has a "foundation in Christian, biblical faith" (p. 86). He does make clear that for this discipleship to be productive it must be enlightened by the Spirit. However, his starting point, or characterization of the "foundation," is what makes his stance more problematic than he recognizes. What exactly does he mean by "Christian, biblical faith"? Later on he is fairly clear that "faith" corresponds to a Christian, or biblical, "worldview." I will leave aside the question for the time being of whether there is such thing as a biblical worldview per se. The notion of such a "worldview" is stock-in-trade these days among evangelical theologians and philosophers, even though I have severely criticized such an assumption in my book *The Next Reformation*.[3] According to Padgett, however, a worldview is something each one of us operates with, and is "handed" to us by our respective "communities" (p. 98). We may start out with a non-Christian worldview in life, but once we have "seen the light" or been convinced by the arguments of Christian apologists, we retool ourselves to function with "Christian" or "biblical" assumptions that constitute in certain respects an operative framework of beliefs. If we are secular in our worldview, we rely on science. If we are Christian, we employ a "theological" mode of reasoning to "improve" our worldview.

Furthermore, "the individual Christian philosopher can and should approach one's own discipline from the broad perspective of a Christian worldview" (pp. 101-2). I assume that this self-improvement course using theological reasoning is what Padgett actually has in mind when

---

[3]See Carl Raschke, *The Next Reformation: Why Evangelicals Must Embrace Postmodernity* (Grand Rapids: Baker Academic, 2004).

he seeks to qualify the relationship between "faith" and "reason." It all comes down to having the right worldview, in the same way that driving from point A to point B requires merely having the right map and knowing, of course, how to read maps. "Thus theology relies upon experts in all the academic disciplines who can rightly interpret the results of other arts and sciences. To find the 'right' interpretation, Christian theology will look to experts who integrate their Christian worldview with the interpretation of results and conflicts in a particular science or philosophy" (p. 103). In other words, Padgett has adopted the standard Catholic perspective that faith should always be "informed" from the outset. In the bygone era of "Christendom" when belonging to some church body was taken for granted and Christian identity was indistinguishable from social participation in the Western world, Padgett's prescription would seem commonsensical. But in an era of acute secularization in the West (even if in much of the world the opposite is the case) the question of faith and reason cannot be boiled down to developing a sophisticated pedagogy for the maturation and refinement of what is assumed to be a Christian "worldview." Scripture is fairly straightforward when it comes to expressing the meaning of what can be understood as faith, and it has little do with merely advancing a Christian "view" of things.

Perhaps the most trenchant characterization of what Scripture means by "faith" can be found in Hebrews 11. Moreover, one of the most pithy, yet hard to translate, renderings can be found in the very first verse of that chapter. "Now faith is confidence in what we hope for and assurance about what we do not see" (Heb 11:1).[4] The term translated in the NIV as "confidence" is *hypostasis*, a common Greek word that goes all the way back to Aristotle. It is placed in apposition with the companion "assurance," or *elenchos*, which can also be construed as "conviction." This "definition" is far more theologically subtle and philosophically sophisticated—at least within the context of the early Christian era when it was written—than biblical commentators down through the ages have often realized. First of all, as the author of *Word Studies in the New Testament*

---

[4]All Scripture quotations in this chapter are from the NIV.

indicates, what strikes us about the author's placement of the Greek word for "faith" (*pistis*) in this verse is the lack of a definite article. It is therefore used "without the article, indicating that it is treated in its abstract conception, and not merely as Christian faith."[5] Clearly, the author of Hebrews is not speaking necessarily to a thoroughly committed, if not catechized, Christian audience who shares his own obvious "Christian worldview." Although the book of Hebrews has been perhaps one of the most difficult texts in the Bible to locate precisely in its historical setting, there is general agreement that it was written for an audience that was experiencing serious persecution and was in danger of committing apostasy, perhaps even reverting to traditional forms of Judaism. The author is employing common Greek philosophical terms, including *pistis*, because he wants to offer a novel and quite distinctive reinterpretation of how our assumptions about the nature of everyday knowledge need revision in light of our response to the person of Christ and the historical reality he represents. The author of Hebrews was "consulting" neither the clerical nor the philosophical experts of his own time to clarify something that was not yet clear. He was deliberately "muddying the waters" of his own generation's common sense in order to make apparent that faith, as contrasted with ordinary philosophical "wisdom," had a truly *revolutionary* meaning for the familiar epistemology of his day. It is because of this intentional stretching and bending of the commonplace usage of certain words or expressions (a technique known in rhetoric as *catachresis*) that the author of Hebrews is providing a unique system of connotations for words like "faith" that still challenge and even puzzle us nowadays.

The Greek *hypostasis* literally signifies something that "stands under" something else. Translated into Latin, the word becomes "substance," an important phrase in both scholasticism and early modern philosophy that implies the enduring reality that underlies fleeting phenomena, or mere "appearances." The twentieth-century philosopher Martin Heidegger, one of the most prominent exponents of the need to "overcome" metaphysics, argued that the familiar spatial imagery in Western phi-

---

[5]Marvin R. Vincent, *Word Studies in the New Testament* (Peabody, MA: Hendrickson, 1985), 4:510.

losophy of a *hypostasis* as a "permanent presence" somehow hidden from
our senses misapplies the original Greek sense of the term as an evident,
nonpropositional intuition of the truth. The habit of recasting such a
truth in propositional, or discursive, terms makes it inevitable that we
would succumb to the spatial imagery of "above" and "below" or "apparent" and "concealed." If we go along with Heidegger, we might best
construe *hypostasis* straightaway as something with *real and immediate
existence*. In Plato's writings *pistis*, or "faith," refers to an inferior or philosophically uncertified pretense to knowledge. When the word occurs,
for example, in Plato's *Republic*, it is usually translated as "opinion."[6]
However, in Hebrews the older meaning is turned upside down. *Pistis*,
or "faith," is a way of knowing that defies common opinion, because it is
a form of personal or existential certitude that has real consequences for
one's life. One knows the "reality" of God without having to demonstrate
his existence, or his personal care for us, philosophically. Faith is not
some prepackaged "worldview" that needs to be further "formed" or
shaped by philosophical inquiry, Padgett's characterization of the theological enterprise. Faith is simultaneously a compelling awareness, a
"conviction," and a call to both action and response that can only be
"demonstrated" by one's own changed life as a "new being" in Christ. The
Greek word in Hebrews 11:1 for those "things" (*pragmata*), of which we
are assured and for which we hope, refers to everything that seems to
defy common sense. In fact, its mode of certification is the fruits of our
faith itself. It embraces "not only future realities, but all that does not fall
under the cognizance of the senses, whether past, present, or future."[7]
In other words, faith does not need philosophy so that we can properly
"adequate" it, as Aquinas would say, to our operative philosophical theories of knowledge. Nor is it something that obviously is discernible as
one element among others of a *community-endorsed* and *tradition-
grounded* Christian theological *worldview*.

In order to grasp this principle all we have to do is read the litany of
the heroes of faith that the author of Hebrews iterates starting in verse 3.

---

[6]Plato's treatment of the term *pistis* can be found in his so-called analogy of the divided line. See
Plato, *The Republic*, 6:509D–513E.
[7]Vincent, *Word Studies*, 4:511.

Each one of these personal stories, or feats, of faith can be seen as derived in some manner from the thesis the author sets forth in verse 2. "By faith we understand that the universe was formed at God's command, so that what is seen was not made out of what was visible" (Heb 11:2). Verse 2 alone is exhibit A that the author of Hebrews sees what we could call "philosophy" as relatively useless in coming to terms with this unique set of insights *and* commitments that we know as faith. Faith gives us a kind of direct knowledge of who God is and what he has in store for us, a knowledge that is only complete once we carry through at the existential level the purpose God has for our new lives, and the aims and goals that our unique obedience to his call has begun to frame for us. This purpose may have nothing at all to do with what our Christian advisers, like Job's friends, tell us in their own smug, self-satisfied style of "consoling" us. As the early church father John Chrysostom put it, "faith needs a generous and vigorous soul" that defies the conventional wisdom, even if it be a "Christian" conventional wisdom. It requires a temperament "rising above all things of sense, and passing beyond the weakness of human reasonings. For it is not possible to become a believer, otherwise than by raising one's self above [the common custom]."[8] When the author of Hebrews that "we understand" (*nooumen*), he is not talking about something that simply strikes the senses as "apparent." "Here is meant the inward perception and apprehension of the visible creation as the work of God, which follows the sight of the phenomena of nature."[9]

The cause-and-effect relationship between the creative power of God's Word and what we experience in a day-to-day setting is not the same relationship that either deductive, or inductive, philosophical reasoning affords us. Even a philosophically embroidered "Christian worldview" that is supposedly consistent with certain theological criteria, or a particular reflective starting point, fails us when it comes to walking, as Abraham did, "by faith." The statement "what is seen was not made out of what was visible"

---

[8]John Chrysostom, *Homilies on the Gospel of St. John and Epistle to the Hebrews*, in *Nicene and Post-Nicene Fathers*, ed. Philip Schaff, series 1 (New York: The Christian Literature Company, 1889), 14:12.
[9]Vincent, *Word Studies*, 4:512.

signifies transparently that the causal connections cannot be ratified by any form of general, or broad-based, "natural" knowledge, let alone the precedents of "scientific" investigation, philosophical methods of inference and beliefs rooted in everyday experience. Only God's future promise, "what is hoped for," can serve as our "evidence."

However, we do not need to wait for this evidence to be obtained. We already have it in our own faith-conviction, one that is even further "substantiated" by the testimony and witnesses of those exemplars of faith, as the book of Hebrews ticks off, that have gone before us. Hence, we need to take with a grain of salt such a statement as the following one by Padgett.

> there is a tradition of Christian scholarship that already seeks to understand all of reality from the perspective of a Christian worldview. While each discipline (like philosophy or biology) will maintain its own standards of good reason, evidence and argument, the Christian will approach her academic specialty from a perspective of faith. (p. 103)

What precisely would be those singular "standards of good reason" that follow from a "Christian worldview," but not necessarily from, say, the physical sciences? Padgett never lays out what distinguishes such a worldview from others, other than the preferred tautology that such a worldview is superior because it is "Christian" or "biblical." This worldview as a surrogate for faith in the biblical meaning is all-encompassing and needs merely to be taken for granted, according to Padgett. It is self-authenticating in its own right; it does not require any unique "faith experience" or special knowledge of God, which classic Christian thinkers associated with the kind of "special revelation" that illumines our heart and produces faith.

> A Christian worldview provides a broad horizon in which the results of research can be interpreted for the larger culture; and . . . when confronted with theories that are currently a matter of intense debate within a discipline, a Christian worldview may sometimes guide the believing scholar in a temporary preference of one theory over another, subject to further review, evidence and argument. The Christian will be guided toward the rival theory or paradigm within a discipline that best fits with her larger worldview, just as any rational being would. This is because we are finally seeking truth, and "fit" with other known truths is an important criterion

in informal reasoning. It may be that, in the long run, our worldview will need to change to fit new facts and theories. (pp. 103-4)

I am rather confounded as to how a Christian "worldview" is so easily open to revision. Does that mean faith itself is easily revisable, depending on the culture we find ourselves inhabiting in any particular generation or age? Is faith a dependent variable of the Zeitgeist? One stumbles in such confusion only if one is trying hard to make faith a form of "knowledge" in the more customary sense of the term, which seems to be not only Padgett's mistake but a whole contingent of contemporary evangelical thinkers who have been hypnotized by the notion that Christian theology must answer to twentieth-century analytical philosophy and its demand that faith be made "reasonable," even if the attempt to do so does not satisfy its would-be antagonists.

Few, if any, philosophers are ever converted to the Christian "worldview" through any methods of persuasion derived from that worldview itself. As the famous story of Paul when he confronted the philosophers at Mars Hill shows us (Acts 17:16-34), the crux of such a Christian "worldview" is the resurrection. "When they heard about the resurrection of the dead, some of them sneered, but others said, 'We want to hear you again on this subject'" (Acts 17:32). The text does not say they were converted by any argument for the resurrection. Indeed, Paul's entire modus operandi in this section was to make the case that the "God of the philosophers," the "unknown" Deity to be apprehended by natural reason, which the ancient Stoics especially affirmed, was indeed the same God whose historical purpose, beginning with and unfolding since the call of Abraham, had been consummated and fulfilled in the events surrounding the life of Jesus. In other words, he is not proffering a sequence of "rational" philosophical inferences from premises to conclusion, but simply claiming to "fill in the blanks" of his audience's own professed ignorance, as his play on the terms "unknown" (*agnōstō*) and "ignorant" (*agnoountes*) emphasize.

The text concludes, of course, that "some of the people became followers of Paul and believed" (Acts 17:34). However, the implication is that they were intrigued by what he was saying because it seemed to "make sense," another way we can render the Greek *episteusan*, rendered in the NIV "believed." They wanted to "hear more," purely and simply, and the only way to do that was to hang out with Paul. But the text is ambiguous about whether they were "convinced" of any argument, which would only happen perhaps if *they trod the way of faith*, to which the risen Christ calls all of us.

The Synthesis of Reason and Faith Response

Craig A. Boyd

ALAN PADGETT PRESENTS A PERSUASIVE CASE for the "faith seeking understanding" perspective advocated by many thinkers in the Christian tradition, including Augustine and Anselm. In many ways, the difference between Padgett's perspective and my own is one of degree rather than of kind. There is a great deal on which we agree. We both see faith and reason—to use his term—as "collegial." We both argue that reason can help illuminate the truths of the faith. Like Padgett, I affirm that neither the Scriptures nor church tradition condemns the use of reason as such, and that we should not be immediately suspicious of philosophy. And we agree that Christian thinkers would do well to consult what contemporary philosophers have to say on matters of faith.

Yet, there is at least one important respect in which we differ. I think reason can play an important role as an antecedent to faith. That is, reason can tell us about some truths that God has "revealed through nature," and we need not always start with the perspective of faith. I do not propose that reason is a "foundation" that faith must build upon but that reason can enable us to see the truths of the Christian faith, since all human cognition is a function of our reason. This does not mean that the truths of the faith can all be subject to the narrow constraints of Enlightenment rationalism. Instead, I argue that there must be some continuity or capacity for the human person to see that the truths of the faith "make sense" in some way to the believer.

To clarify, Padgett does not say that reason itself is inoperative prior to faith but that "what I reject is the idea that one will always set the stage for the other in *interdisciplinary* work" (p. 86). This is an interesting claim and seems to resonate with his idea that faith has a certain kind of priority over reason. But what notion of reason does he reject? I think there is an ambiguity in his use of the term and that once we clarify the ambiguity we can see how his views differ from my own.

So how should we use the term *reason*? As I have argued, there are at least three ways in which we can construe the term. Reason[1] is the idea that reason can only function in a very narrow philosophical, or empirical, sense. In this way, we see the logical positivists and others who would see reason as a welcome—and objectively justified—alternative to the allegedly spurious claims of faith. One can see that the law of non-contradiction—"A is not non-A"—is true for all people at all times in all places. This a priori truth does not alter according to varying geographical or temporal conditions. For reason[1] the undeniable truths of reason stand in contrast to the claims of faith. When one considers the idea that "God has forgiven my sins," one seems to have no objective criterion to make an appeal for the truth claims of this assertion. Is it analytically true or empirically verifiable? The thinkers who advocate the sole use of reason[1] like to contrast faith and reason with the purpose of showing that reason is the preferable choice. After all, there have been "wars of religion," but we do have to look very hard to find "wars of reason." On this view, reason is an unqualified good.

In contrast to the "high view" of reason advocated by many analytic philosophers, we have the perspective of many thinkers in the Reformed theological tradition who see themselves following in the tradition of the later writings of Augustine, Luther and Calvin. These thinkers view reason with suspicion. In his later years, Augustine's controversies with the Pelagians led him to emphasize grace and faith at the expense of nature and reason. Luther famously called reason a "whore." And Calvin's views on the fall of all humanity led him to mistrust reason as a guide to any salvific knowledge. Reason[2] is the view that reason—like all other human capacities—is tragically and fatally fallen. Here the idea is that one should not trust in philosophy, as it will hold one "captive" to worldly beliefs and principles (Col 2:8). And after all, Abraham was "saved by faith" and this was "reckoned to him as righteousness" (Rom 4:3 NRSV).

My own position is that we should adopt an understanding of reason that takes into account the full range of human capacities. This view sees the limitations of what can be known by any creature, yet it also insists that these limitations do not undermine reason's usefulness. It is how the human creature comes to understand, process and decide how to live one's life given the multiform ways in which reality can be apprehended and the ways in which we are shaped by competing narratives. Reason[3] operates before, during and after one's conversion. It can, of course, be used for nefarious purposes, but reason can also guide an individual into the truth by discerning true from false narratives and by seeing the need for redemption and subsequent sanctification in light of God's grace.

These rational functions should not surprise us. In his treatment of the natural law Aquinas points out that all people know that they should "pursue the good and avoid evil" and that they should "acquire virtue."[1] There operates in every human being (1) a desire to become a better person and (2) the knowledge that we are not the persons we could be. There is a teleology to our nature that beckons us beyond our current selves.

The fact that many of us want to go to college, to become physically fit, to rid ourselves of unhealthy eating habits, to develop meaningful friendships and to become persons of character speaks to the fact that we have— at least implicitly—an inborn desire to be better. It is difficult to see how this basic desire could be so corrupted that it could or should be rendered inoperative. John Wesley called this basic desire "prevenient grace" because it directs all believers to the goodness of God. It is that "first grace" we find in John 1: "from his fulness we have all received, grace upon grace" (Jn 1:16 NRSV). But we must also insist that this grace is "natural" to us and not an alien intruder into our lives. We not only have this basic desire to be better persons but also know that we can be better and we can recognize the good when we see it. Reason grasps who we are, what we can be and the need to move from the former to the latter.

Faith, according to Padgett, is a "kind of trust" that is central to the development of both philosophy and theology. The empiricist as well as the theologian needs to practice a kind of "trust" in what her senses tell her. Here we see the continuity between faith and reason that fideists— such as Rashcke—deny. In addition to this helpful suggestion, Padgett also sees thinking and trusting as activities of the "whole" person—not

---

[1]Thomas Aquinas, *Summa Theologiae* 1-2.94.2.

merely functions of specific elements of the soul, so to speak. That is, there are affective and cognitive aspects in both thinking and believing. Reason, as such, is not set up against faith but is complementary to it. But Padgett cautions: "Reason is a gift of God, but it is not the highest aspect of our existence" (p. 91). It, like anything else, can become an idol or used for evil purposes. Faith, however, is focused on the person and work of Jesus Christ and, as such, is not capable of being misused. Religion and religious institutions can be misused, but not genuine faith in Christ.

Padgett says that "Christian theology should be grounded in the gospel of Jesus Christ, and so in the Scriptures and in the great classical tradition of historic Christian faith, as well as the identity-forming practices of the church" (p. 107). As a Christian I have no argument with that statement. If Christian theology fails to make Jesus Christ central then it fails to be Christian theology. Certainly reason can—and should—be employed in the service of Christian theology. But Christian theology is a narrower slice of the "faith and reason" pie. The scope of faith and reason extends beyond the articles of faith to other areas such as the interplay of science and faith, what can be known about God by means of our unaided natural reason and what the study of literature can contribute to our understanding of the Christian Scriptures, just to name a few topics.

But why is this important? If we turn to Thomas Aquinas we see that reason can inform all people about God to a degree. He says that we can know that God is one, that God is the Creator of the universe and that there are some basic moral principles all humans know "naturally." These truths are called *praembula fidei*, or "preambles to the faith."[2] These truths are not articles of faith proper but truths that can either be proved rationally or taken on faith, depending on an individual's capacity to think philosophically. Aquinas believes that some people can prove that God exists and that there is only one God, but he admits this is extremely difficult and time-consuming. In either case, one's reasoning comes to grasp (1) what reason can know, (2) the limits of one's own reason and (3) that the truths of the faith are not contrary to faith. In any case, it is

---

[2]Thomas Aquinas, *Summa Contra Gentiles* 1.4.

important to note that Aquinas uses "reason" in more than one way.

Reason can refer to the ability one has to think philosophically and to engage in philosophical argumentation according to those truths that are known by the natural light of reason. For example, he refers to the fact that there are "divine truths that surpass human reason."[3] These truths are the mysteries of the Trinity, the incarnation and so on.

Reason, however, can also refer to the generic capacity to think about any topic at all or even the capacity to grasp a concept or make a judgment. Here reason is employed in both philosophical and theological disciplines. This is what Aquinas calls *scientia*. This is an intellectual virtue or a discipline that employs the intellectual virtues in its pursuit of truth. But the virtue of *scientia* is "right reasoning about things that are known." What this statement shows is that even in theology—which takes as its starting point the revealed truths about God—right reasoning is ever present and can be understood as "the starting point" of any kind of human inquiry.

Padgett quotes Lossky favorably when the Russian thinker claims that "no philosophical speculation has ever succeeded in rising to the mystery of the Holy Trinity" (p. 109). This is certainly true. However, it does not mean that an understanding of the unity of God is at odds with the mystery of the Holy Trinity. I am not here claiming that Padgett makes this assertion, but I want to point out an important feature of the synthesist's position. Certainly, there are mysteries that unaided human reason can never penetrate; even with the help of divine grace some mysteries, such as the Trinity and the incarnation, can only be apprehended and not comprehended. That is, we can grasp the difficulty of understanding the mystery even though we cannot grasp the mystery itself in its own fullness. Reason plays an important role here in both (1) demonstrating its own limitations and (2) helping to articulate what the mystery means. The Trinity, for example, is not contrary to reason but is "above" reason. That is, it extends beyond the scope of reason's grasp, and reason itself recognizes this.

While reason's powers recognize that they are insufficient to discover

---

[3]Thomas Aquinas, *Summa Contra Gentiles* 1.4.

the reality of the Trinity by its natural powers, once known through revelation, reason still has a vital role: it can help us understand the nature of the Trinity as far as any creature can understand the Creator. This combines Aquinas's second and third definitions of reason mentioned above. Even if faith's truths are *above* reason such that they are not discoverable by our unaided natural reason alone, they are *not contrary* to faith. While Padgett suggests that applying reason's faculties to trinitarian doctrine is valid, the theologian Jürgen Moltmann provides a concrete example of how reason expresses the coherence of revealed truths. Moltmann points to our recognition that there can be no genuine love without authentic community. All of reality, and indeed all of life, he says, "is community in communication."[4] Thus reason can draw upon this observation to help us grasp the logic of God as Trinity. If God is a relational being whose defining attribute is love, our understanding of community illuminates what the divine life of the Trinity must be like to a degree. Thus Moltmann describes the activity of the Trinity in the following manner.

> By virtue of their [the persons of the Trinity] eternal love they live in one another to such an extent, and dwell in one another to such an extent, that they are one. It is a process of most perfect and intense empathy. . . . The "circulation" of the eternal divine life becomes perfect through the fellowship and unity of the three different Persons in the eternal love.[5]

It is only because reason grasps the ideas of "circulation," "fellowship" and "community" that we can understand the Trinity. Reason, operating as a guide, prepares the way for such theological apprehensions.

As I see it, Padgett's views and my own are not that far off. What I want to emphasize is that reason is always and everywhere operative. Even in interdisciplinary work, reason operates prior to our development of other ideas and concepts. As a result we can, with Aristotle and Aquinas, say that human beings are "rational animals."

---

[4]Jürgen Moltmann, *The Trinity and the Kingdom: The Doctrine of God* (San Francisco: Harper & Row, 1980), p. 175.
[5]Ibid.

3

The Synthesis of Reason and Faith

Craig A. Boyd

INTRODUCTION

IN 1615 THE AMBITIOUS JESUIT PHILOSOPHER Paulo Foscarini decided to publish a treatise defending the view that Copernicanism (the idea that the earth and the other planets orbited the sun) was consistent with the Christian faith. Up until this point in history, the commonly accepted view of the cosmos was the Ptolemaic view: the idea that the sun, the moon, the other planets and the stars all orbited the earth, which remained stationary. This older, Ptolemaic view of the cosmos was one that most in the Roman Catholic Church also embraced. However, Foscarini was not a lone voice crying in the wilderness. Another, more famous scientist, Galileo Galilei, also shared his view. Furthermore, Galileo set out to demonstrate that the newer model was true and that the older model, although intuitively more plausible, was wrong.[1]

Galileo claimed to have good reasons for believing the earth orbited the sun. Even though the earth did not appear to move (except for during earthquakes), with the use of a telescope one could see moons orbiting Jupiter and could observe that Venus appeared to go through phases, as our moon does. These data proved, at the very least, that not all objects in the heavens orbit the earth. That is, Galileo could falsify the Ptolemaic cosmology, but he could not confirm Copernicanism.

Foscarini's treatise, which supported Galileo's views, provoked one of the most powerful men in the church at the time, Cardinal Robert

---

[1]For an overview of the Galileo affair see Richard J. Blackwell, *Galileo, Bellarmine, and the Bible* (Notre Dame, IN: University of Notre Dame Press, 1991).

Bellarmine, who advanced three reasons why the church should not accept the Copernican model. First, it violated common sense. The earth does not feel as if it moves about the sun, and the sun appears to move across the sky. Second, the Copernican model seemed to violate the Holy Scriptures themselves. God had "established the earth upon its foundations from which it will not be moved" (Ps 104:5).[2] And on one occasion Joshua told the sun to "stand still," and it did (Josh 10:13). How could the sun stand still if it weren't moving about the earth? Third, the theory not only irritated the philosophers and theologians of the day but also stood in direct contradiction to the consensus of the fathers of the church. Clearly, this was a pernicious, and possibly irrational, theory that the church should not endorse. The upshot was that the church declared the Ptolemaic cosmology to be the correct view, but the Copernican model—while it could be used for calculating the calendar—was not to be understood as representing the way the universe truly operated.

This historical conflict between Galileo and Foscarini on the one hand and the Roman Catholic Church on the other has provided so-called defenders of reason with what seems to be a ready-made example of how religion irrationally defends dogma while science calmly and reasonably promotes the pursuit of truth unencumbered by useless religious ideas.

Yet as we have seen in the Galileo vignette, it was Foscarini, a priest, who was one of the first to support Galileo. To argue, as some have, that the church unanimously sided against Galileo and in support of religious dogma is simplistic and factually wrong. Rather, the Galileo affair, as it has come to be known, happens to be an isolated case of some in the church who got it wrong. Even so, it raises important and difficult questions for those who would affirm reason ("science" being one particular expression of reason) and faith.

Many Christians consider "reason" a problem they need to overcome. After all, doesn't God require "belief" and not intellectual dexterity? Isn't it better to "believe" than to "know"? And aren't we expressly warned by

---

[2]All Bible references in this chapter will be to the New Revised Standard Version.

Paul to "See to it that no one takes you captive through philosophy and empty deceit, according to human tradition, according to the elemental spirits of the universe, and not according to Christ" (Col 2:8)? Contemporary conflicts between atheists and believers only serve to exacerbate the apparent gulf between faith and reason, with each side appealing to the claim that its views are "rational" and the other side's views are not. So is Christian faith rational? Irrational? Or something else?

In this essay, I argue that that the best way to view the relationship between reason and faith is as a "synthesis" of the two. God has endowed human beings with rational capacities, and these capacities can, and do, lead us to truth. However, these rational capacities do not, and cannot, by themselves offer us salvation. In calling my view a "synthesis," I intend to appeal to the tradition of Christian thinkers who trace their own views—either directly or indirectly—to the work of Thomas Aquinas. These thinkers include, among others, Richard Hooker, John Wesley, John Henry Newman, Etienne Gilson and C. S. Lewis.[3]

The "faith and reason" discussion seems to rely on a more basic "grace and nature" relationship. How we navigate these concepts usually determines how we understand faith and reason. In order to understand the synthesist's views on faith and reason, we will look first to an explication of the relationship between nature and grace. If nature is evil, and reason is an aspect of nature, then reason must also be evil. But if nature is the creation of a good God, then it must also be good. We can see, therefore, that "nature" (as well as many other concepts we employ) is a "mediated" concept. That is, it brings a great deal of intellectual baggage with it, and so our first task is to unload the baggage and sift through the contents.

---

[3]See Thomas Aquinas, *Summa Theologiae* (Rome, Leonine edition, 1873–1976) (all translations are the author's), and *Summa Contra Gentiles*, vol. 1, trans. Anton C. Pegis (Notre Dame, IN: University of Notre Dame Press, 1975); Richard Hooker, *Of the Laws of Ecclesiastical Polity*, ed. A. S. McGrade (New York: Cambridge University Press, 1989); John Wesley, "An Appeal to Men of Reason," in vol. 11, and "The Origin, Nature, Purpose, and Use of the Law," in vol. 2 of *The Works of John Wesley*, ed. Gerald Cragg and Albert Outler (Nashville: Abingdon, 1987); Etienne Gilson, *Reason and Revelation in the Middle Ages* (New York: Charles Scribner's Sons, 1936); C. S. Lewis, *Mere Christianity* (New York: Macmillan, 1952); Lewis, *The Abolition of Man* (New York: Macmillan, 1947); Lewis, *The Problem of Pain* (New York: Macmillan, 1962); and Lewis, *Miracles* (New York: Macmillan, 1960).

NATURE

For our purposes I want to consider at least three different constructions of the term *nature*. These three different meanings reflect (1) an "empirical" understanding of nature that emphasizes the characteristics of the world around us; (2) a particular theological understanding of nature that appeals to the radical distinction between the categories of corrupt nature and redeeming grace; and (3) a metaphysical understanding of the term that captures the important elements of the empirical but also considers an important teleological dimension that certain animals, especially humans, may have. That is, it appears that animals—especially humans—act for the sake of an end or purpose (telos). And so on this last view of nature—the more philosophical view—we interpret our world as having design and purposes for which various beings act. To summarize, nature can be understood as:

nature[1]: the object of various scientific inquiries that focuses upon explanations of how natural objects and living beings act and are acted upon.

nature[2]: a principle of corruption resulting from a primeval fall of humanity wherein the active power of nature is contrasted with the restorative powers of grace.

nature[3]: the fulfillment of the natural telos embedded in humans in creation; it includes but is not reducible to nature[1].

Nature[1] has its roots in modernist conceptions of the sciences. Scientists in various disciplines ranging from biology to physics posit an intelligible "nature" that can be categorized, studied and manipulated in order to understand the mechanisms of various objects. This view of nature focuses more on the mechanisms of how natural objects and organisms function in their appropriate environments and less on the teleological questions of why they developed in this or that particular way.

Nature[2] has been primarily associated with Reformed and fideist thinkers who see in the Bible a contrast between nature and grace. These thinkers see nature as a principle of corruption that has resulted from Adam's fall. On this view nature is a dubious category since it is "fallen" and therefore untrustworthy as a source of knowledge.

Nature[3] is the view of those Christian metaphysicians who mediate between the views of those who see nature primarily as the fallen creation of a good God and those who see it as a merely empirical construct. These thinkers view nature as an ontological category (i.e., a category that addresses more than how a being behaves) that seeks also to discern its essential telos, or purpose. Hence, it is known as the synthesist view, because it retains important commitments from nature[1] and nature[2] but also transcends both views as it develops a more fully articulated and comprehensive metaphysic. Philosophers and theologians who appeal to nature[3] include Aristotle, Cicero, Paul, Augustine and Aquinas, who all held that to understand a thing required more than merely knowing its parts and how it works. Rather, nature included an ontological dimension that could not in principle be reduced to mere mechanism but always appealed to some divinely ordained purpose operating within the agent.

GRACE

The choice of how to engage correlative theological concepts reveals a great deal about the hidden assumptions one may bring to the discussion. If one starts with a grace-sin axis, the assumption is that these concepts are the twin poles between which all important theological questions arise. It further presupposes that sin is the primary category that defines human nature and that sin must be overcome, destroyed or defeated by grace. I do not wish to say that sin is not an important theological category, but I do contend that it is parasitic upon other more basic categories—namely the goodness of God and the goodness of the created order, what we might also call nature[3].

For the synthesist, nature has a certain kind of continuity with its original state since it reflects the goodness of God. It has been damaged by sin, but it retains its created integrity. Nature is not something to be overcome or destroyed but completed, perfected or healed. One of the key ideas in the synthesist's view is that "Grace does not destroy nature but perfects it."[4] But how is it possible for the natural order to be both fallen and possess a basic integrity at the same time?

---

[4]Aquinas, *Summa Theologiae* 1.1.8.

Suppose I purchase an old house in the historic section of St. Louis. Over the past 130 years it has suffered from neglect, the elements and the natural decay that any structure would experience. But the foundation is still good, and the oak beams that form the skeleton of the house are much stronger than anything built today. Although the house could provide some shelter from the dreary Midwestern winters and the unbearably humid summers, it is not "what it should be." It's not the place I would want to move into without making some improvements first. So I begin the remodeling project.

I put a new roof on the house and apply new siding to the exterior. I replumb the sinks, toilets and baths. I install new electrical circuits, refinish the floors and paint all the interior walls. The project has capitalized on the basic structural integrity of the house, repaired the decaying elements and replaced those elements that were beyond repair. The home has been "restored," not "destroyed." The house is now recognizable as being the house "as it should be."

In a similar way, divine grace perfects or heals nature. That nature is never destroyed since the basic integrity of the creation remains. In fact, if that "nature" did not remain we could not coherently speak of that thing or person. When we speak of an object, we want to know "what it is"—that is, we want to know its nature since its nature is what it fundamentally is. But even when those natures undergo change they do not cease to be what they most fundamentally are. That is, I contend that what we are is more basic to us than the condition in which we find ourselves.

The upshot of this is that sin is always parasitic on something more basic and has no reality in and of itself. That "something more basic" is nature. Sin affects our nature like time and the elements affect the house that stands in need of repair. "Disrepair" is not a thing in itself but a condition of something else, something more basic: the house. So too, sin is a condition of something more basic: human nature. As a result, grace does not destroy our nature—which includes our rational capacities—but makes us "what we should be" while retaining our most basic integrity as human persons. In a very important sense, our humanity trumps our sinfulness.

Just as a house cannot repair itself but must rely on some other agent, so too a human being needs divine grace to restore and heal the damages of sin. This, of course, does not mean that sin is unimportant. Rather, what we want to say is that even though sin separates us from God and one another and harms our very being, the grace of God is greater than the power of sin. The same God who created us does not destroy us but enables us to become the persons we were meant to be.

The synthesist's view of faith and reason appeals to the prior relationship of grace and nature.

Grace	as	Faith
Nature		Reason

Just as nature[3] has its own integrity that requires the healing perfection of grace, so too reason has an integrity of its own that stands in need of faith in order to be "what it should." Yet reason can still grasp that it is, in itself, insufficient to the task.

COMPETING DEFINITIONS OF REASON

In a now-famous volume on virtue ethics, philosopher Alasdair Mac-Intyre asks the question—which also serves as the title of his book— "Whose Justice, Which Rationality?"[5] The answer concerning justice depends upon a prior conception of reason. What exactly do we mean by "reason"? Once we can answer this question adequately, we can move on to discern what the relationship is between reason and faith. As I see it, there are at least three ways in which we can see reason operating that correlate to the three definitions of nature we developed above.

reason[1]: is the attempt of the human creature to use science and logic to understand reality as given to our senses and our natural capacity to see inferences and relationships

reason[2]: is the sinful attempt of human creatures to demand that reality conforms to their prior expectations and limited perspective on reality apart from divine revelation

---

[5] Alasdair MacIntyre, *Whose Justice? Which Rationality?* (Notre Dame, IN: University of Notre Dame Press, 1988).

reason[3]: is how the human creature comes to understand, process and
decide how to live one's life given the multiform ways in which reality can be apprehended and the ways in which we are shaped by
competing narratives.

These three definitions are not necessarily mutually exclusive, but they
do point to ways in which reason has been appropriated by both philosophers and theologians. As I see it, reason[1] is not simply wrong but
incomplete. Reason[2] represents an understandable but misguided attempt to view all "reasonable enterprises" as doomed from the start.
Reason[3] will be the one I defend as most consistent with the Christian
tradition of the synthesist.

Reason[1]. Philosophers as diverse as Aristotle and Kant saw reason as
the capacity to know and understand the ways in which the world works.
Reason investigated the relationships between and among various entities
and accordingly made appropriate kinds of judgments. Reason was a
somewhat value-neutral capacity that all humans possessed. It is difficult
to see how this capacity in itself represents a threat to Christianity. Indeed,
it was the use of these capacities that led Galileo to make his famous and,
at the time, controversial judgments concerning the solar system.

If we look closer at Galileo's predicament we see that he appealed to
the well-known principle of "right reason." For the ancient, medieval and
Renaissance thinkers this was a capacity to know and judge. It also included the ability to make appropriate inferences, which were known as
"demonstrations." Galileo stood at the juncture between Aristotelian logic
(and science) and the early modern empirical methods. Although it is
easy for us to contrast the two and claim that Aristotle was simply wrong
about so many things (e.g., the idea that all material reality was composed of the four elements air, earth, fire and water), there is a genuine
continuity between the ancient and early modern notions of reason.
Both believed that reason could discover basic truths about the world
and that these truths could and should be corrected in the light of new
evidence. There is nothing intrinsically anti-Christian in any of this.
However, as time went on new ways of conceiving how reason should
operate in normative ways began to threaten the faith.

The Enlightenment significantly altered our understanding of "reason" in the modern/postmodern world. With the work of John Locke we see the starting point of the Enlightenment understanding of reason as "liberated" from the domain of faith. The tradition follows through to Immanuel Kant and up to the twentieth century's analytic philosophy. Just as the Peace of Westphalia (1648) put an end to the European "wars of religion," so too Enlightenment philosophy promised an end to seemingly interminable theological debates by appeals to reason and science.

Analytic philosophers picked up on this tradition, and we can see it at work in G. E. Moore's *Principia Ethica*, Ludwig Wittgenstein's *Tractatus Logico-Philosophicus* and (most clearly) in A. J. Ayer's *Language, Truth and Logic*.[6] In this work, Ayer famously appealed to something called the "verificationist principle," which held that for any statement to have meaning it must be either analytically true or empirically verifiable. For example, if I say, "The Chicago Cubs won the 1908 World Series," this is a historic event that we can verify empirically. That is, we can find records of the event in newspapers, journals and other sources. In a way, we "look and see" whether the assertion is true. Or in a similar way, I could determine that the statement "Charlie is a dog" is true by observing that she has fur, mammary glands and gives birth to live puppies. In both cases I appeal to empirical evidence to determine whether the statement is true and has meaning.

Yet some statements are meaningful because they are analytically true. By virtue of the meaning of the terms we know that they have meaning. If I say, "A bachelor is an unmarried male," this statement has meaning simply because the subject is strictly identified with the predicate term.

The upshot of the application of the verificationist principle was that analytic philosophers determined that subjects such as ethics and theology (near and dear to the hearts of theists everywhere) were meaningless utterances. Since ethical and theological claims were neither analytically true nor empirically verifiable they must, therefore, have no meaning. Since God was traditionally defined as an "immaterial substance," and since immaterial substances could not be empirically

---

[6]A. J. Ayer, *Language, Truth, and Logic*, 2nd ed. (New York: Dover, 1956).

verified, any talk of God had to be dismissed as meaningless. There simply was no referent for God. So too any discussion of a soul, free will or the miraculous would all have to be seen as meaningless. The meaninglessness problem, however, extended beyond traditional theological problems.

Any talk of "the good" or what constituted "the right" was also meaningless.[7] If I were to say, "It was wrong for Jean Valjean to steal the bread," the word "wrong" has no empirically verifiable meaning (and stealing is clearly not a priori wrong given the meaning of the terms). There is no "empirical quality" that terms such as "wrong" and "right" can refer to.

Ethics and theology, for these analytic philosophers, were set aside for the more important work of clarifying concepts and ideas that could be analyzed in terms of logic. But just as importantly, "empirical verification" led philosophers to engage the empirical sciences more seriously. Although logic and interdisciplinary engagement with the sciences were not bad in themselves, many saw this linguistic—and by implication, ontological—restriction on philosophical inquiry as the worst sort of reductionism conceivable since every term must have an empirically verifiable referent. The result was that this type of reduction essentially collapsed faith—and its content—to a sphere that was entirely separate from the realm of reason and quarantined religious notions to one's personal life and mere preferences.

What sounded the death knell of the logical positivist's verificationist principle is that the principle itself is unverifiable. The central tenet of logical positivism was neither analytically true nor empirically verifiable but had to be accepted on "faith." This became a source of embarrassment for analytic philosophers. However, there was a deeper problem that most of these analytic philosophers failed to grasp.

The concept of reason itself was not simply an unmediated idea. That is, reason is not, as the Enlightenment philosophers before them had held, a concept or faculty that everyone understood in a manner similar to understanding geometric axioms. Who were those privileged few who got to define this most important of concepts? Why were the positivists

---

[7]Here, however, analytic philosophers saw a need to recover "ethics." Theology, though, did not seem to merit such interest.

somehow the only ones gifted enough to see how philosophy really worked? These questions led philosophers such as Alasdair MacIntyre to observe that there are "traditions" or "narratives" of reason.[8]

Yet while logical positivism began to fade from respectable philosophical circles, it gained new traction among scientists who latched onto the idea that (1) the only genuine knowledge we could have was scientific knowledge, and (2) the only real entities populating the world were those that could be discovered by these empirical means.[9] This approach, widely known as "scientism," seeks to usurp the place of traditional philosophy by replacing it with "science." Richard Dawkins and E. O. Wilson have both advocated the idea that science should now be the arbiter of all that is and all that can be known.[10]

For Dawkins, religion (as well as traditional philosophy) has failed to sift the meaningful from the meaningless. Instead of helping us to see what is and what has value, religion has propagated war, crime, superstition and every evil under the sun. One of his most popular accusations is that religion (and faith) is a "virus."

> It is fashionable to wax apocalyptic about the threat to humanity posed by the AIDS virus, "mad cow" disease, and many others, but I think the case can be made that *faith* is one of the world's great evils, comparable to the smallpox virus but harder to eradicate. Faith, being belief that isn't based on evidence, is the principal vice of any religion. And who, looking at Northern Ireland or the Middle East, can be confident that the brain virus of faith is not exceedingly dangerous? One of the stories told to the young Muslim suicide bombers is that martyrdom is the quickest way to heaven—and not just heaven but a special part of heaven where they will receive their special reward of 72 virgin brides.[11]

---

[8]Alasdair MacIntyre, *After Virtue: A Study in Moral Theory* (Notre Dame: University of Notre Dame Press, 1981).

[9]Mikeal Stenmark, *Scientism: Science, Ethics, and Religion* (Burlington, VT: Ashgate, 2001). Stenmark says there are four distinctive theses: "T1 The only kind of knowledge we can have is scientific knowledge. T2 The only things that exist are the ones science can discover. T3 Science alone can answer our moral questions and explain as well as replace traditional ethics. T4 Science alone can answer our existential questions and explain as well as replace traditional religion" (p. 18).

[10]Richard Dawkins, *The Selfish Gene*, new ed. (Oxford: Oxford University Press, 1989); Edward O. Wilson, *Consilience: The Unity of Knowledge* (London: Little, Brown, 1998).

[11]Richard Dawkins, "Is Science a Religion?," *The Humanist* 57, no. 1 (1997): 26.

Dawkins also accuses those who propose to inculcate religious principles in their own children of "child abuse" since they substitute clear thinking based on "reason" and "science" for dangerous superstitions that promote ignorance and hatred of others. On his account, all acts of terrorism, barbarism, inequity and moral depravity can be traced to religion.

Wilson, although more modest in his rhetoric, basically agrees with the idea that science alone provides the only narrative that can piece together the disparate disciplines and unify them into a coherent whole. Biology can provide the "consilience" that can unify the academic disciplines. In his famous work *Sociobiology*, he makes the bold claim that "scientists and humanists should consider the possibility that the time has come for ethics to be removed . . . from the hands of the philosophers and biologicized."[12] The idea here is that the traditional humanities, such as ethics, should be subsumed under biology since the sciences provide us with "truth" while the humanities are merely subjective (i.e., "mere faith") attempts at providing us with genuine knowledge. Scientism can be seen, therefore, as the reduction of all disciplines to the metanarrative of "science."

Scientism thus represents the worst abuses of reason[1] because it takes the natural desire to investigate the world and extends it beyond its proper scope. Scientists, as such, do not ask philosophical questions. They examine evidence, collect data, make hypotheses and work within the limits of empirical research. They ask, "What took place at the big bang?" But they don't ask, "Why was there a big bang in the first place?" Dawkins betrays this basic understanding between the sciences and the humanities when he naively asks,

> So where does life come from? What is it? Why are we here? What are we here for? What is the meaning of life? There is a conventional wisdom which says that science has nothing to say about such questions. Well all I can say is that if science has nothing to say, it's certain that no other discipline can say anything at all. But in fact science has a great deal to say about such questions.[13]

---

[12]Edward O. Wilson, *Sociobiology: The New Synthesis* (Cambridge, MA: Belknap Press of Harvard University Press, 1975), p. 262.
[13]Richard Dawkins, in *Growing Up in the Universe*, BBC Education (video series), 1991.

The fact is, science has nothing to say about any of these questions unless, of course, we equivocate on the meaning of the word *science* and conflate it with *scientism*. We can pose an argument against this particular manifestation of scientism in the following way:

1. Science, as such, is not metaphysics.

2. But those who practice "scientism" want to make metaphysical claims such as "Science discovers all that is there."

3. But if those who practice "scientism" are going to "do metaphysics," then they should come out and say that is precisely what they are doing.

Henry Plotkin claims that those who work in the empirical sciences often move from their own empirical disciplines into metaphysics without the slightest hesitation (and without understanding) of considering the philosophical claims they are making. Plotkin writes,

> Underlying all the biological and social sciences, the reason for it all, is the "need" (how else to express it, perhaps "drive" would be better) for genes to perpetuate themselves. This is a metaphysical claim, and the reductionism that it entails is . . . best labeled as metaphysical reductionism. Because it is metaphysical it is neither right nor wrong nor empirically testable. It is simply a statement of belief that genes count above all else.[14]

It is this apparent attempt to use reason against religious belief that has caused many to see reason[1] as a threat.

Reason[2]. Many devout Christian thinkers have rightfully distrusted those who would employ philosophical arguments against the Christian faith. This suspicion dates back to the earliest times in Christianity, from Tertullian down through Bernard of Clairvaux to Søren Kierkegaard. These thinkers have not seen reason as an ally to faith but as a competitor. Reason on this view is a fallen faculty of a fallen creature.

The theological tradition that emphasizes the utter sinfulness of humanity and the primacy of belief is known as fideism. Here we see the glorification of faith and the denigration of reason. This approach takes two

---

[14]Henry Plotkin, *Evolution in Mind: An Introduction to Evolutionary Psychology* (Cambridge, MA: Harvard University Press, 1998), p. 94.

different forms: the textual and the existential. The "textual fideist" sifts through the Bible looking for passages that would appear to support her own preconceived biases, while the "existential fideist" considers the extent and intensity of his own sin as the dominant narrative of his own existence.

The textual fideist considers passages such as Colossians 2:8 as normative for the Christian life. These passages are quoted out of context and brandished as "proof" that God does not want anyone studying philosophy. Other passages praising the "foolishness of the gospel" and the "foolishness of the cross" (1 Cor 1:18) and denigrating the "wisdom of the world" (1 Cor 3:19) are also invoked to support the idea that God doesn't like philosophy. This more simplistic form of fideism we shall leave to the side as it hardly represents the best of the fideistic tradition.

The existential fideist poses a more serious objection to the role that reason can and/or should play in the life of the believer. On this view, one does not merely pick and choose biblical passages that seem to call into question the nature of philosophy or of reason, but one mounts theological arguments against the use of reason. There are at least two approaches: the more radical fideist (as represented by thinkers such as Kierkegaard and Tertullian) and the more moderate fideist (as represented by Augustine).

The more radical fideists believe in a total corruption of the human mind. These thinkers hold to a notion of sin that so thoroughly permeates the human creature that there can be no good thing, apart from the radically transformative grace of God, that the human creature can accomplish on her own. The argument runs in the following manner:

1. All humans are corrupted by sin.

2. All aspects of humanity are corrupted by sin.

3. Reason is an aspect of human nature.

4. Thus reason is radically corrupted by sin.

From this point the radical fideist argues that anything the human creature can "know" must also be corrupted. The only source of genuine knowledge must therefore be through the revelation of God (either in terms of a personal encounter or mediated through text or tradition). As a result, the radical fideist sees the relationship between faith and reason as one of conflict. One cannot serve two masters.

The key problem here is self-referentialism. That is, any attempt to refute reason that explicitly or implicitly appeals to the hearer's own reason is self-refuting. The only thing a radical fideist can say is "Believe!" No argument can or should be made. If we admit even the most basic argument, we are assuming the validity of some element of "reason" that has not been damaged by the fall and this runs counter to their most basic belief: that all of humanity is corrupted by sin. However, there is a more persuasive form of fideism that seems more "reasonable."

The more moderate fideist sees the relationship between faith and reason as one of priority. It is not the case that reason has no part to play, but that it must be relegated to a secondary status. The moderate fideist agrees with the radical fideist on the priority of faith. One can do no good thing apart from the grace of God. Yet the moderate sees grace as having a restorative power on reason. One can use reason *in defense of* the faith even though one cannot reason *to* faith. The moderate fideist reasons as follows:

1. All humans are sinful but can be transformed through grace.

2. Reason, as an aspect of human nature, is sinful but can be transformed by grace.

3. No one, prior to grace, can be transformed.

4. Thus reason can only function as it should after the restorative work of grace.

Augustine demonstrates how this works in his famous *Commentary on the Literal Meaning of Genesis* when he says that Christians who do not possess understanding of both the Scriptures and how nature works ought not to propose silly ideas to intelligent nonbelievers. He says:

> The shame is not so much that an ignorant individual is derided, but that people outside the household of the faith think our sacred writers held such opinions, and, to the great loss of those for whose salvation we toil, the writers of our Scripture are criticized and rejected as unlearned men. If they find a Christian mistaken in a field which they themselves know

well and hear him maintaining his foolish opinion about our books, how are they going to believe those books in matters concerning the resurrection of the dead, the hope of eternal life, and the kingdom of heaven, when they think their pages are full of falsehoods on facts which they themselves have learnt from experience and the light of reason?[15]

The key to understanding this passage is that reason can inform all people about the basics of the cosmos. The truths of science are accessible to anyone who possesses "the light of reason." As a result, Christians who understand neither the Scriptures nor science should keep quiet because they "bring untold trouble and sorrow upon their wiser brethren."

For Augustine, as for most of the moderate fideists, reason plays its role in service to faith. That is, salvation serves as the motivation for engaging the unbeliever. They need to know God and have communion with God. Thus for anyone to present absurd ideas to unbelievers damages the opportunity for their salvation. Reason clearly operates in the lives of unbelievers in ways that are legitimate. Yes, the Christian must employ reason to (1) get the foolish Christians to stop their nonsense and (2) to persuade the unbeliever that the Christians are not foolish. But why can we only employ reason in the service of faith? Can't it function, to some legitimate extent, without special revelation or the prior gift of grace?

Reason[3]. I have claimed that reason[3] is how the human creature comes to understand, process and decide how to live one's life given the multiform ways in which reality can be apprehended and shaped by competing narratives. In a sense, it is a more inclusive understanding of what reason does rather than a narrower, more theological or empirical notion.

Those of us who advocate for reason[3] have to start with the idea that *any* human activity proceeds from human "reason." That is, whether I am remembering my daughter's birth, planning a trip to New Zealand, learning to play the ukulele, repenting of my sins or contemplating the beauty of the Pacific Ocean, each one of these acts is an act of reason. But I should be quick to point out that reason and rationality are not the same thing. Those of us who live with the tradition of the Enlightenment tend

---

[15] Augustine, *Commentary on the Literal Meaning of Genesis*, trans. John Hammond Taylor (New York: Newman Press, 1982), 1:43.

to see rationality as something beginning with Descartes in his attempt to find philosophical certainty and eradicate doubt. This, however, is a specifically philosophical sense of the term—one that would contrast rationality with faith. In order to recapture a more adequate understanding of the term we might again consult the views of Thomas Aquinas.

For Aquinas, reason was a rich and analogous notion. The Latin word *ratio*, when properly understood, is a far cry from what we mean today by rationality or reason. For Aquinas, a *ratio* was an expression of relationship. To reduce it to a notion of syllogistic logic, linguistic clarification or a specifically philosophical method of demonstration would be absurd. Indeed, it is our *ratio* that enables us to see all sorts of relationships: parent-child, wife-husband, creature-Creator, friend-friend, steward-environment and so on. It certainly does include analyzing syllogistic logic, parsing Greek sentences and distinguishing strict identity statements, but it does much more than that.

But what exactly does reason do? It apprehends, it judges and it engages in discursive processes. That is, we find that the mind begins with apprehension, which enables us to perceive a thing. But we never perceive something as just a "generic thing"; we always perceive it as a particular kind of thing. And so the mind also judges that the apprehended object is what it is and not something else. Finally, the mind can reason from effects to causes and from causes to effects. These three acts of reason are common to all human beings and need no special act of grace in order to operate. The atheist and the theist can both apprehend and judge that the object before them is a dog. They can also reason that if they do not move quickly the snarling dog will likely bite them. Once again, it is by the "natural light of reason" (to use Aquinas's phrase) that we can all grasp this.

The synthesists all hold that "the natural light of reason" can enable us to engage in agrarian and artistic ventures, the natural sciences and mathematics, grammar, logic, and rhetoric and quite simply the "daily affairs of life," to use John Wesley's phrase.[16] These are all very helpful and practical matters, and no one, after even a little reflection, can deny that

---

[16]John Wesley, "The Case of Reason Impartially Considered," in *Wesley's Works* (Peabody, MA: Hendrickson, 1990), 6:355.

all people—regardless of their own particular faith—can do these things. Yet reason has at least two other functions: it discovers basic moral truths and facilitates the understanding of the Christian faith.

Everyone knows some basic truths about ethics regardless of their own faith tradition or even lack of a faith tradition. In the opening pages of his book *Mere Christianity*, C. S. Lewis makes this appeal to reason as the first step in his argument for God's existence. He says:

> Everyone has heard people quarrelling. Sometimes it sounds funny and sometimes it sounds merely unpleasant. . . . They say things like this: "How'd you like it if anyone did that to you?"—"That's my seat, I was there first."—"Leave him alone, he isn't doing you any harm"— . . . People say things like that every day, educated people as well as uneducated, and children as well as grown-ups.
>
> Now what interests me about all these remarks is that the man who makes them is not merely saying that the other man's behavior does not please him. He is appealing to some kind of standard of behaviour.[17]

Lewis refers here to the tradition of natural law: the idea that all people intuitively know some basic moral truths about right and wrong. And if this is so it must be that God can, and does, communicate to us in intelligible ways.

What Lewis hits on here is that there must be a basic congruity between our use of reason and the way the reality truly is. If God does not communicate to us in ways appropriate to our ability to know anything, then the universe truly is absurd. It must be the case that a child's feeble first attempts at a drawing a wheel must, in some primitive way, be congruent with God's understanding of a perfect circle. Simply because there is a difference between the way that we and God apprehend or understand the nature of a circle, it does not follow that these ideas are incommensurable. Lewis elaborates further when he considers the continuity between God's moral judgments and our own.

> If God's moral judgment differs from ours so that our "black" may be His "white," we can mean nothing by calling Him good; for to say "God is good," while asserting that His goodness is wholly other than ours, is really

---

[17]C. S. Lewis, *Mere Christianity* (New York: Macmillan, 1952), p. 17.

only to say "God is we know not what." And an utterly unknown quality in God cannot give us moral grounds for loving or obeying Him. If He is not (in our sense) "good" we shall obey, if at all, only through fear—and should be equally ready to obey an omnipotent Fiend. The doctrine of Total Depravity—when the consequence is drawn that, since we are totally depraved, our idea of good is worth simply nothing—may thus turn Christianity into a form of devil-worship.[18]

If God cannot communicate to our "unaided reason," then no one could come to understand God's commands to us (since we employ reason in every act of human understanding). But clearly people do understand the basic commands of God to us (e.g., "Do not murder," "Do not lie" and "Treat others as you would have them treat you"). So God can, and does, communicate to our "unaided reason." As a result, the claim that reason can do no work prior to divine revelation must be rejected. In fact, we should say that reason is a critical element involved in any human understanding of God since divine communication to us presupposes that we possess the capacity to understand who God is and what God requires of us.

FAITH

Faith is an ambiguous term, and so it makes sense to clarify what it is and what it is not. Consider the following three statements:

1. The earth travels in an elliptical orbit around the sun.

2. Galileo was an obnoxious human being.

3. God is love.

The first statement is a judgment of knowledge. Once I know something about gravitational forces, the relative mass of the earth and the sun, the nature of planetary objects, and the definition of an ellipse, my intellect judges the statement to be true. I do not "believe" it to be true; I know it to be true. My intellect is forced to conclude the truth of this statement.

The second statement is a judgment of opinion. I read about Galileo

---

[18]C. S. Lewis, *The Problem of Pain* (New York: Macmillan, 1962), pp. 37-38.

and his volatile relationships with others. I consider the rhetorical tone of his correspondence with people, and I weigh this "evidence" and conclude that he was probably an annoying person. This is my opinion, and my intellect is not "forced" into making this judgment; I choose this as a reasonable idea. But the data I gather comes from various sources that may or may not represent Galileo accurately and so my opinion about Galileo is much less certain than my judgment about the earth's orbit.

The third statement is a judgment of faith. I accept the idea that God is love because it has been revealed by God. It is, of course, possible that I may be deluded or that I don't understand the meaning of the term "love" or that I am blindly following the mimetic tendencies of my culture. That is, the truth of the statement is not based upon an analytically true definition or empirically verifiable data. Rather, I believe it based upon the trustworthiness of the source: God.

Faith is, therefore, a commitment to belief based upon the testimony of God. Although this helps clarify what faith is not, there remains some ambiguity. Typically we think of faith meaning three different things: faith as content, faith as act and faith as habit.

Faith as content refers to the actual content of what people believe. Here people who "have faith" believe that God is a Trinity, that Christ rose from the dead, that their sins are forgiven and that the righteous will inherit eternal life, as well as other such notions. This kind of faith is sometimes referred to as "*the* faith," meaning all those propositions that the Christian community assents to.

Faith as act refers to an individual act of faith. This kind of faith is a mental assent to the truth of some particular statement. If I say "I believe in the Trinity," what I mean is that I give a mental assent to that notion that God is three persons. This is an act of belief. But isolated "acts of belief" are not what constitutes the daily life of the believer.

Faith as habit refers to the continuing belief patterns of a person. My beliefs do not suddenly appear and disappear in an entirely erratic fashion. Rather, I develop "patterns of believing." This kind of faith is a "theological virtue." Lewis writes, "We have to be continually reminded of what we believe. Neither this belief nor any other will automatically remain alive in the mind. It must be fed."[19] But this kind of faith can never be separated in principle from our capacity to engage in continuous thoughtful reflection. In other words, faith requires a kind of continuous critical reflection not only on the content of the belief but also on the ways in which we believe.

One of the key descriptions of faith from the Bible is found in the epistle to the Hebrews: "Now faith is the assurance of things hoped for, the proof [or evidence] of things not seen" (Heb 11:1). This famous passage simultaneously emphasizes both the psychological certainty the believer possesses—in the "assurance of things hoped for"—as well as the uncertainty inherent in faith—in the "things not seen." This seems to reflect what Aquinas says about "faith"; there is the certainty found in the person in whom we believe combined with the fact that our intellect is not forced to assent to its truth. Rather, we choose to believe. Yet that choice to believe does not depend entirely on the choice itself. What we see is that there is "evidence for things not seen." If faith were a sheer act of choice, there would be no need for evidence. But what role does evidence play in the life of faith?

As we have seen, the fideist believes that faith is its own justification. That is, the fideist contends that arguing for God's existence or trying to provide a rationale for why one believes what one believes never produces faith itself. When one "proves" God's existence, one no longer "believes." Kierkegaard subscribed to this view and claimed that it is the uncertainty of faith that makes it faith. "Without risk there is no faith," he wrote. "Faith is precisely the contradiction between the infinite passion of the individual's inwardness and the objective uncertainty. If I am capable of grasping God objectively, I do not believe but precisely because I cannot do this I must believe."[20] That is, unlike the Copernican view of the cosmos, God's existence cannot be "proven." Oddly enough, this lack of proof is not a vice but a virtue. Still, one is left with some important questions: How exactly does one determine how to believe? Is belief its own justification? And if so, will just any belief serve since all criteria seem to have been eliminated?

---

[19]Lewis, *Mere Christianity*, p. 124.

[20]Søren Kierkegaard, *Concluding Unscientific Postscript to* Philosophical Fragments, trans. Howard V. Hong and Edna H. Hong (Princeton, NJ: Princeton University Press, 1974), p. 182.

In contrast to the fideist, an "evidentialist" claims that one's beliefs—even if they are not scientifically demonstrable—are subject to some kind of reasonable inquiry. The extent to which someone bases his beliefs on reason will determine the degree to which we can call him an evidentialist. That is, if every belief he has must be grounded on "sufficient evidence" then he would hold a form of "strong evidentialism." W. K. Clifford once famously proclaimed that "It is wrong, always, everywhere, and for anyone to believe anything upon insufficient evidence."[21] On this view, no one could hold any religious beliefs at all since to do so would violate Clifford's principle, which invoked empirical evidence for its justification.

In contrast to this extreme view, we could find another view more closely allied to the fideists according to which beliefs merely need to be "properly basic."[22] The beliefs themselves are not based on evidence per se, but the idea here is that we all have some ideas that need no further evidence. And if we were to trace every belief we hold to some prior evidence, the search would go on indefinitely. So it may be that our belief that God exists is a basic belief that needs no further justification, just as my memory of my vacation in Michigan in 2001 needs no further justification.

FAITH AND REASON

In his attempt to persuade the defenders of the old Ptolemaic cosmology, Galileo appealed to the idea that there are two "books: the 'Book of Nature' and the 'Book of Scripture.'" Clearly, for him, the church guided the people in an understanding of the "Book of Scripture" (since for a layperson to do so was tantamount to heresy in a post-Reformation Catholic world). But God also communicates to us through the natural order. Galileo wrote:

> Philosophy is written in this grand book, the universe, which stands continually open to our gaze. But the book cannot be understood unless one first learns to comprehend the language and read the letters in which it is

---

[21]William K. Clifford, "The Ethics of Belief," in *The Rationality of Belief in God*, ed. George Mavrodes (Englewood Cliffs, NJ: Prentice-Hall, 1970), p. 159.

[22]Alvin Plantinga, "The Reformed Objection to Natural Theology," *Christian Scholar's Review* 11 (1982): 187-98.

composed. It is written in the language of mathematics, and its characters are triangles, circles, and other geometric figures without which it is humanly impossible to understand a single word of it; without these, one wanders about in a dark labyrinth.[23]

Without taking the time and effort to study the world as it ought to be studied, one cannot truly grasp the brilliance of God's work. And yet, this "book" does not contradict the other "Book," because God is the author of both books. That is, God both creates and reveals; and there is no contradiction between the special revelation of God in the person of Jesus Christ (or in the Bible) and the divine order that God shows to us in creation. God is the source of both sorts of communications—otherwise we have a schizophrenic God as well as a worldview that is at odds with itself. As Aquinas says, "It is impossible that the truth of faith should be opposed to those principles that the human reason knows naturally."[24] And this is because God is the author of human reason as well as the author of Holy Scripture. The reason Galileo (and Augustine and Aquinas and many others) say this is because of the principle of the unity of truth. According to Mortimer Adler, "All the diverse parts of the whole truth must be compatible with one another regardless of the diversity of ways in which these parts of the truth are attained or received."[25] One could easily substitute "truth discovered by reason" for "scientific truth" and the meaning would be preserved.

The principle applies not only as a help for unraveling problems that seem to arise between science and faith but also those that appear among the various scientific disciplines themselves. No biologist will ever be heard to say, "Well, that may be true in physics, but it's plainly false in biology." This is because all empiricists want to say that judgments that are true, when properly contextualized, will not contradict judgments in other disciplines. Or at least, if they seem to, we always assume that they are in principle resolvable. This notion applies more broadly to the issue

---

[23]Galileo, "The Assayer," in *Discoveries and Opinions of Galileo*, trans. Stilman Drake (New York: Anchor, 1957), pp. 237-38.

[24]Aquinas, *Summa Contra Gentiles* 1.7.

[25]Mortimer Adler, *Truth in Religion: The Plurality of Religions and the Unity of Truth* (New York: Macmillan, 1990), p. 105.

of truths known by reason and truths believed by faith. Aquinas makes the claim that

> There is a twofold mode of truth in what we profess about God. Some truths about God exceed all the ability of the human reason. Such is the truth that God is triune. But there are some truths which the natural reason is also able to reach. Such are that God exists, that He is one, and the like. In fact such truths about God have been proved demonstratively by the philosophers, guided by the light of natural reason.[26]

These truths that faith reveals to us are not contrary to reason but "consistent with" or "above" reason. There is a deep continuity between what we can know about God through nature and what we can know about God through special revelation. The key to this continuity is the divine *logos* that gives to all humans the "natural light of reason."

Aquinas claims that this natural light of reason operates in each and every human intellect and that we see it not only in our ability to understand the ways in which the world around us works but also in our grasp of the "natural law." All people know basic truths about morality. He says that the "natural law is the rational creature's participation in the eternal law."[27] This expression highlights an important element for the synthesist, because it is a reference to the second person of the Trinity. The "eternal law" is identified with the *Verbum Dei*, that is, the "Word of God," the divine *logos*, the preincarnate Christ.[28] He serves the dual role as the Author of the book of nature as well as the Author of the book of revelation.

The natural light of reason is a kind of participation in the eternal law. It enables us to know basic truths about the created order, including empirical notions such as heliocentrism, as well as moral principles, such as the prohibitions on stealing and murder. This participation in the eternal law provides both ontological and epistemological advantages for the synthesist's view of faith and reason, because the divine *logos* is himself the eternal law. God is identified with the eternal law.

In questions concerning the relation of creatures to God, participation

---

[26] Aquinas, *Summa Contra Gentiles* 1.3.

[27] Aquinas, *Summa Theologiae* 1-2.91.2.

[28] Aquinas, *Summa Theologiae* 1-2.93.1.2.

has an ontological dimension. All created beings owe their existence, goodness, unity and specific characteristics to the creative activity of God. According to Aquinas, "'To participate' is, as it were, 'to grasp a part'; and therefore, when something receives in a particular way that which belongs to another in a universal way, it is said 'to participate' in that."[29] Obviously, humans receive their nature from God and participate in God's creative activity.

The *imago Dei* is what bridges the ontological and epistemological gap that would seem to separate the human and the divine. Aquinas says, "A person is called the image of God, not because one is essentially an image, but because the image of God is impressed upon one's mind; as a coin is the image of the king, as having the image of the king."[30] This image is such that humans imitate God by acting on the basis of knowledge and with freedom. He says, "That the human is made to the image of God . . . implies that the human agent is intelligent and free to choose and govern oneself."[31] There is a sense in which humans imitate God—in their own finite capacity—by being responsible for their own behavior. Freedom and knowledge provide the sine qua non for responsible action. Since humans participate in divine reason by being created according to God's image, they are also thereby enabled to understand why God gives the commands God gives and to see the essential rationality of the natural law.

The divine image in humanity is seen most clearly in the human capacity to reason. This is what distinguishes human life from all other forms of organic life. Although these other forms also participate in the eternal law, the human creature does so in a more excellent way. By means of reason, we know, we deliberate, we choose and we engage in purposive activities. All of this is accomplished by the natural light of reason bestowed in creation.

---

[29] Aquinas, *An Exposition of the "On the De Hebdomads" of Boethius*, trans. Janice L. Schultz and Edward A. Synan (Washington, DC: Catholic University of America Press, 2001), p. 19.

[30] Aquinas, *Summa Theologiae* 1.93.6.1. It is important to note that Aquinas speaks of the human person being made "to the image of God" (*ad imagine Dei*) since it is only in Christ that we see the perfect image of God. The idea conveyed here is that the image in human persons is a *movement toward* God.

[31] Aquinas, *Summa Theologiae* 1-2, prologue.

All things are said to be seen in God, and all things are judged in him, in as much as it is by *participation* in his light that we know and judge all things. For the very light of natural reason is a *participation* in the divine light. So also we are said to see and judge of sensible things in the sun, that is by the sun's light. . . . Just as in order to see a sensible thing it is not necessary to see the substance of the sun, so in a similar way to see something intelligible, it is not necessary to see the essence of God.[32]

The natural light of reason enables us to know the nature of any created being. This ability that all human beings possess includes knowing various elementary truths about God, the natural world and the basic elements of morality. Although explicit knowledge of God is not required to understand the world, God makes that knowledge possible by creating humans *ad imagine Dei*. Aquinas reiterates this when he says that "Every knowing of truth is an irradiation and *participation* in the eternal law."[33]

Since the preincarnate Christ (i.e., the Word) is the eternal law, it follows that every act of cognition on the part of a human creature is a participation in the creative power of God. Although this may sound like an Augustinian theory of "divine illumination," it is not. Aquinas thinks we have the natural ability to see secondary causes (e.g., laws of nature such as gravity, procreation and life cycles) at work in creation by means of an essentially empirical approach to the world. Even though there are obviously Platonic ontological elements in his consideration of the eternal law, the means by which one comes to know the formal nature of any being is by means of Aristotelian epistemology unaided by any kind of special revelation. Otherwise, atheists and agnostics could not know anything about the world, and it is manifestly clear that they do.

The capacity to know basic truths about the natural world and the basic truths of morality provides an unexpected benefit when it comes to asking to what extent our belief in God's goodness is rational. That is, without the proper use of reason[3] it would be impossible for us to know and love God. MacIntyre has observed, only a just (and good) God is owed obedience. Therefore, we must distinguish between the true God (i.e., the

---

[32]Aquinas, *Summa Theologiae* 1-2.12.11.3. Italics added for emphasis.
[33]Ibid., 1-2.93.2.

omnibenevolent God who is worthy of worship) and those that are pre-
tenders (e.g., the ancient Roman's Jupiter or William Blake's Nobodaddy).
But how could we do this if we did not possess some a priori capacity to
know "the good"? In order to do this, we must have a basic knowledge of
the good before we can judge which God ought to be obeyed.[34]

But how is this possible? Aquinas believed that all humans, by virtue
of the natural light of reason, apprehend the good. This apprehension is
made possible by the fact that humans are made *ad imagine Dei*. Yet this
apprehension of the good is not an exhaustive knowledge of the good,
but a basic conception that has its basis in God. In question 2 of the
prima pars, Aquinas presents the famous "Five Ways." These are five
ways by which he believed we can "demonstrate" the existence of God.
These "proofs" are not widely accepted today by philosophers as demonstrations of God's existence, but rather they are ways in which we can
think about how and why God would be a plausible explanation for the
existence of all that is. Richard Swinburne says, "The argument to God
from the world and its regularity is, I believe, a codification by philosophers of a natural and rational reaction to an orderly world deeply embedded in the human consciousness."[35] Or in more Thomistic terms, we
could say that the arguments for God's existence are simply the means
by which the natural light of reason leads us to think that there is a God
who created and designed the universe.

The "Fourth Way," the proof for God's existence from the degree of
perfections, appeals to precisely this idea of the continuity between
human and divine conceptions of goodness. Aquinas says:

> Among beings there are some more or less good, true, noble, and the like.
> But "more" and "less" are predicated of different things according as they
> resemble in their different ways something which is the maximum. . . .
> Now the maximum in any genus is the cause of all in that genus. . . .
> Therefore there must also be something which is to all beings the cause of
> their being, goodness and every other perfection; and this we call God.[36]

---

[34]Alasdair MacIntyre, "Which God Ought We to Obey and Why?" *Faith and Philosophy* 3
(1986): 364.
[35]Richard Swinburne, *Is There A God?* (New York: Oxford University Press, 1996), p. 54.
[36]Aquinas, *Summa Theologiae* 1.2.3.

Here we see the natural light of reason at work, moving from the lower degrees of perfection found in created beings to the uncreated "maximal" perfection of goodness found in God. If there wasn't this continuity then no knowledge of God, or of the good, would be possible. Humans seem to be created with a capacity to apprehend the good that enables them to perceive the different degrees of perfection in various creatures and to posit a divine source of all that is good. We are supposed to be able to recognize goodness, and even a hierarchy of goodness, prior to concluding the existence of God. However, it is precisely from such a vision of things that the existence of God becomes manifest, where the term *God* means the maximal cause of all goodness and being.

Since humans are created in the *imago Dei* and since this image is never lost, even though sin disrupts and distorts our thinking, there is a basic continuity between what we can know by means of the creative work of the *verbum Dei* and the redemptive work of the incarnate Word. Our conception of goodness determines the manner in which God meaningfully can be said to be "good." Our conception of goodness is not a product of our own hubris; it is a product of reflection on the nature that God has created and that is available to all who would consult it. There is thus continuity between our ideas of goodness, as creatures made in the image of God, and the commands that God gives.

The difficulty Aquinas sees in humans is not one of moral knowledge but of the disorder of the will. Moral knowledge comes to humans by means of both natural and special revelation. As he says, "A person cannot even know truth without divine help. . . . And yet, human nature is more corrupted by sin in regard to the desire for the good than in regard to the knowledge of truth."[37]

CONCLUSION

It is a mistake to assume that reason is ever "unaided" by divine grace since it was created by divine grace and—although damaged by sin—never fully loses its efficacy. Our nature is more stable than the harmful effects of sin. As a result, all people can know basic truths about the

---

[37]Ibid., 1-2.109.2.3.

world, God and morality. Regardless of religion, all people can reason correctly about the various operations of the natural world and the basic elements of morality as found in the natural law. Aquinas (and many others) acknowledged that reason can show us that there is a God—these are what he calls the "preambles" to the faith. That is, we can know that there is a God, but this, in and of itself, does not make us "Christian."

Reason can also come up with reasons for rejecting God as well as rationalizations for our immoral behavior. Merely employing our rational faculties does not make us good or evil. At one point Aquinas tells us, "Nothing is intrinsically good or evil but the manner of use makes it thus." What he means by this is that the end we intend functions as the primary cause of our activity. (This does not mean, however, that the "end justifies the means" in every case but that it is the only thing that can justify our actions.) Reason, like any other faculty, can focus on the love of God or the love of self or the love of any other created good. As a result, our attention must be directed to the goodness of God as our primary end, and it is divine grace that enables us to do this.

The revelation of God in Christ—and in the Scriptures—points us to the reality that our efforts alone cannot produce the love of God that we need to order our lives rightly. We all stand in need of that divine grace that perfects but does not destroy nature. Reason directs us to a good that we cannot achieve by our own efforts. Like Moses, it can see the "promised land" and know how to get there but it does not have the resources to make the journey alone. Reason not only recognizes the need for grace but is also healed by that grace.

A "reason" that is healed by grace is one in which its original integrity has been restored and can also help explicate the meaning of such items as the incarnation, the Trinity, the forgiveness of sin, the resurrection of the body and other mysteries of the faith. Though we should not expect complete comprehension of these ideas, since they are mysteries, we can have some apprehension of what they mean and how they should function in our lives. Yet this use of reason is not some kind of hubris wherein we are searching into forbidden territory but the gift of God to be used and employed in the service of faith.

Faith and Philosophy in Tension Response

Carl A. Raschke

BOYD OFFERS AN INCREDIBLY RICH and far-ranging account of the compatibility of faith and reason on what is at the same time a remarkably broad philosophical canvas. He comes close to pushing me to reassess my own Protestant convictions and embracing what might be charitably called a "postmodern Thomism." He has also persuaded me that even though I adhere, as do all Christians in some measure if they are true to their own version of the tradition, to the "priority" of faith over reason, I am not a "fideist" in the stereotypical sense, even though I understand the word to be more clearly delineated in its implications than Boyd would desire. It occurs to me that the term "moderate fideist" is comparable to "somewhat pregnant." In other words, it suggests that we can ascribe magnitude or gradation to something that is absolute in its essential meaning and hence unqualifiable.

At the same time, Boyd is right on when he assails the sort of dogmatism of empirical reason, or "scientism" as he calls it, most evident in the logical positivists and today's rabid critics of "religion" such as Christopher Hitchens and Richard Dawkins. Scientism is just another type of reductionism, which both ignores and appears to be ignorant of the complexity of both the history of science and the scientific method as a whole. When it is wearing its full-blown ideological colors and adopts the kind of take-no-prisoners attitude that the so-called new atheists exhibit, it can easily be dismissed as just a peculiar species of secularist fundamentalism that is barely distinguishable from Islamist terrorism or those who seek to bomb abortion clinics.

Boyd seems to be of the view that in many ways the fanaticism of the scientist critics of Christianity is simply the flip side of the Reformation suspicion of natural reason, which Martin Luther, the father of Protestantism, termed a "prostitute." "By nature and manner of being she is a noxious whore; she is a prostitute, the Devil's appointed whore; whore eaten by scab and leprosy who ought to be trodden under foot and destroyed, she and her wisdom."[1] John Calvin, who was heavily influenced by Renaissance humanism, took a less extreme position without the rhetorical fireworks of Luther, yet at the same time he regarded natural reason as something blinded and depraved because of the fall of Adam. Natural reason has its proper sphere, albeit a very limited one. The problem arises when one seeks to use these corrupted natural powers to acquire the "knowledge of God," which he considered blasphemy and insanity. "The earth sustains on her bosom many monster minds," Calvin wrote in his *Institutes of the Christian Religion*, "minds which are not afraid to employ the seed of Deity deposited in human nature as a means of suppressing the name of God. Can anything be more detestable than this madness in man?"[2] In retrospect, we can view the Reformers' hostility to the use of natural reason in the theological enterprise as a reaction to the excesses of late medieval Catholic scholasticism, which drew on the subtleties of Aristotle's method of logical argument to make extravagant claims about matters of faith and God's workings in both this world and in the heavenly realms.

For the Reformers, the only reliable knowledge of God we can have comes from Scripture, which is God's unique "special revelation." Boyd, in contrast and in a twentieth-century cry of "enough" to the mainline Reformation tradition, wants to salvage the earlier Thomistic view of reason by reshaping it in a distinctive twenty-first-century context, drawing to some extent on the insights of the present-day natural sciences themselves. He wants to see the faith/reason relationship as analogous to the Thomistic distinction between grace and nature. Boyd characterizes such a perspective as one that "synthesizes" faith with reason, a term he takes directly from the Thomists themselves. "Nature has a certain kind of continuity with its original state since it reflects the goodness of God. It has been damaged by sin, but it retains its created integrity. Nature is not something to be overcome or destroyed but completed, perfected or healed" (p. 135). It is, of course, in the Thomistic

---

[1]Martin Luther, *Works*, Erlangen Edition (Philadelphia: A. J. Holman, 1915), 16:142.
[2]John Calvin, *Institutes of the Christian Religion*, trans. Henry Beveridge (Grand Rapids: Eerdmans, 1989), 1:53.

picture divine grace that does the "perfecting" or "healing." However, Boyd asks, "How is it possible for the natural order to be both fallen and possess a basic integrity at the same time?" (p. 135). Boyd gives the illustration of an old house that has fallen into disrepair, which someone buys, remodels and restores. "The home has been "restored," not "destroyed." The house is now recognizable as being the house "as it should be" (p. 136).

Boyd argues, in effect, that both the Reformers and the new atheists as noisy partisans of "scientism" have thrown the baby out with the bathwater. The Reformers rejected as a consequence the classical Christian view that natural reason is part of the order of creation, and that our efforts to exercise it within its proper parameters are a form of stewardship, not pride and arrogance. After all, as the story in Genesis of the Garden of Eden shows us, God did not forbid knowledge, only the quest for an absolute and ultimately destructive form of knowledge represented in the image of the "tree of the knowledge of good and evil" (Gen 2:7 NIV). If we can venture a contemporary reading of this powerful story that for centuries has been the center of theological reflection and artistic renderings, it is that God blesses us with a desire and a curiosity to come to know those things that are truly of him and that, as the Reformers put it routinely, "profit" us. This kind of knowledge is epitomized in the "tree of life," which according to the Genesis account God sets alongside the tree that grows the forbidden fruits. In other words, God created us not only with "free will," as Christian doctrine has always stressed, but also with the capacity for discernment and proper judgment, what Boyd terms "right reason," following the terminology of the early modern era in theology.

Scientism would argue that we can routinely depend on this natural ability to make judgments about the nature of things, independently of any special knowledge of God, whose existence and of course whose divine prohibitions about delving into the spaces of forbidden knowledge they deny. The Reformation stance, on the other hand, can be summarized as follows. Human beings had their chance to use their reason responsibly in the garden, and they "blew it." As an example, no responsible parent would allow their teenager to drive the family car right away if on the teenager's first unaccompanied outing he or she took it to have a drag race with their friends, got drunk, and crashed and overturned it. The parent would insist that their child demonstrate the proper maturity and perhaps take further driver education until they could be trusted to take the vehicle out once more. For Calvin, it was Christ's saving intervention on our part, and the "sanctifying" role of the church, that saved us from the dread consequences of Adam's initial "bad decision." But we cannot be really trusted with the "car"—that is, the use of natural reason—until the world is restored finally and eschatologically.

In his commentary on Genesis Calvin makes some observations about this primordial "bad decision" that retain some serious implications still today. Calvin notes that the "fall" was not so much an act of deliberate disobedience on the part of Adam and Eve so much as a failure of rationality itself from the very beginning, the power of deduction that was given to the first humans as a consequence of their ability to speak and to engage in dialogue and "reasoned" discourse.

> Now the serpent was more crafty than any of the wild animals the LORD God had made. He said to the woman, "Did God really say, 'You must not eat from any tree in the garden'?"
>
> The woman said to the serpent, "We may eat fruit from the trees in the garden, but God did say, 'You must not eat fruit from the tree that is in the middle of the garden, and you must not touch it, or you will die.'"
>
> "You will not certainly die," the serpent said to the woman. "For God knows that when you eat from it your eyes will be opened, and you will be like God, knowing good and evil." (Gen 3:1-5 NIV)

According to Calvin, Satan enters into the snake, which in the first chapter of Genesis is created as part of the "good" order of things, and engages in a very subtle type of beguiling reasoning—what today we would term "sophistry"—so that he might "deceive more covertly, would gradually proceed with cautious prevarications to lead the woman to a contempt of the divine precept." In other words, even in the Garden the problem is not so much Eve's defiance, or willfulness, but her ingenuous trust of another natural creature, which she is unable to discern has been "possessed" by the Adversary, along with an innocent misuse of her God-given ability to think sequentially and logically. Calvin writes: "I have no doubt that the serpent urges the woman to seek out the cause [of the command], since otherwise he would not have been able to draw away her mind from God. Very dangerous is the temptation, when it is suggested to us, that God is not to be obeyed except so far as the reason of his command is apparent."[3]

In the Greek philosophical tradition from Aristotle forward the basis of philosophical reasoning is the search of fundamental "causes" (*aitia*) that, once obtained, provide the seeker with a deeper "wisdom" (*sophia*). Philosophy itself is the "love of wisdom" (*philo-sophia*).[4] Thus the entire framework for the operations of reason (*logos*) rests on this demand for causal explanation. Instead of accepting God's command, as anyone who intimately trusted their maker would be expected to do, Eve demanded a more elaborated and satisfying intellectual "justification," with which the serpent was more than happy to oblige her. As she pursued the philosophical "dialogue" (*dia-logos*, or "reasoned exchange") with the serpent, the innate tendency toward the distortion of the meaning of God's original, unexplained injunction became apparent. If reason could not be trusted in its very first exercise in the entirety of the human story, could it ever be trusted? As the famous psychoanalyst Sigmund Freud pointed out, we often confuse our own seemingly "sound" arguments with our the perverse logic of our hidden wishes, and we can always come up with good "reasons" for just about anything, a process he termed—borrowing a term from contemporary Ernest Jones—"rationalization."[5]

Rationalizations, a synonym in ordinary speech nowadays for "making excuses," constitute a very nuanced way of convincing ourselves, not to mention others, of things we are not supposed to have or do by offering a set of qualifying conditions that make our previous hesitation, which may be the genuine voice of conscience, seem less valid or compelling. That is exactly how the serpent "deceives" Eve in

---

[3]John Calvin, *Commentary on the First Book of Moses Called Genesis*, trans. John King (Grand Rapids: Christian Classics Ethereal Library, 2005), 1:96.
[4]This argument can be found in the first two sections of book 1 of Aristotle's *Metaphysics*.
[5]See Sigmund Freud, *Three Case Histories* (New York: Macmillan, 1963), p. 179.

the first five verses of Genesis 3, and how Eve in turn further augments the deception because of her curiosity about "why" she should not do what God strictly forbade her to do. As any parent knows, the best way to get a child to do something you really do not want them to do is to say simply "don't do it" without offering a reason. The child will then, unless they completely fear the parent, start asking the proverbial question of *why*, and if the parent falls into the trap they will end up in endless argument with the child until, in exasperation, they will finally say, as my father always did, "Because I'm Father, and I told you so." Of course, that was for me an invitation to "rationalize" why I should go ahead and do it behind his back. The point of Genesis, as Calvin notes in his own characteristically flamboyant and rhetorical manner, is that this tendency to "rationalize" is not merely God's punishment on the human race for having disobeyed him. It is a flaw of reason itself, which like a dangerous weapon can easily and often quite inadvertently be terribly misused.

We do not want necessarily to belabor the Genesis example. But one way of interpreting the example in the context of the question of the proper range of activity for both faith and philosophy is to recognize that if you are going to use reason when it comes to the things of God, proceed with great caution. What is most obvious about the simple but enthralling tale of Eve's encounter with the snake, the mask of Satan, is that it all came down to whom she really trusted. Faith, as the Hebrew word *'ĕmûnâ* suggests, really means the kind of personal and intimate knowledge of something that is founded on assurance or "trust." Eve took God for granted, and she decided that the "dialectical" reasoning of the serpent was more convincing than the authority of her own Creator. The bottom line was that God said *not* to eat of the tree, and after "rationalizing" her desire to go against God's authority, she made the contrary authority. What God was forbidding, in effect, was the desire for "wisdom," what comes across metaphorically in the biblical text as the "knowledge of good and evil." Another way of translating the Hebrew is "knowledge of everything there is." That rendering corresponds in certain respects to the Greek *sophia*, which may be construed also as the "fundamental reasons why things are as they are." Later on this aim of philosophy to push the knowledge of causes to the absolute limit came to be regarded as the discipline of "metaphysics."

Did God forbid the desire for metaphysical knowledge? Not necessarily. Aristotle said that all human beings "desire to know." But, as the great eighteenth-century philosopher Immanuel Kant (whom some regard as the greatest of all Western philosophers and who was also a committed Christian) reminded us, metaphysics has its strict boundaries, and we should only exercise philosophical reason when we are mature and humble enough to recognize the boundaries of reason. Kant's monumental work *The Critique of Pure Reason* was designed to put the pretensions of metaphysics in their place and to use reason to demonstrate the limits of reason. In the preface to the second edition of *The Critique of Pure Reason*, Kant wrote that it is necessary "to abolish *knowledge* in order to make room for *faith*."[6] It is both telling and a little ironic that a philosopher of such stature who sought to warrant the proper use of rationality would prioritize not reason itself but "faith." A true faith, Kant insisted, is indeed a "rational faith," but it is first and foremost faith nonetheless. What did Kant have in mind exactly?

Let us return to the Garden of Eden story. As Kenneth Matthews, writing in the New American Commentary on Genesis, puts it, the primal pair "obtained 'wisdom' in exchange for death."[7] Twentieth-century philosophers from Martin Heidegger to Ludwig Wittgenstein have been preoccupied with the question of death. But for them the question does not concern so much what happens, if anything, in the

---

[6]Immanuel Kant, *Kritik der reinen Vernunft* [*Critique of Pure Reason*] (Köln, Germany: Anaconda, 2011), p. 43. Translation from the original German mine. This famous passage has been translated in various ways over the years in different editions. A recent one, for example, is the Doubleday edition based on the nineteenth-century translation by Max Müller. "I had therefore to remove *knowledge* in order to make room for *belief*." *Critique of Pure Reason*, trans. Max Mueller (New York: Doubleday, 1966), p. xxxix. The German word *aufheben* that is translated here as "remove" is better translated as "abolish," as is common in earlier English versions of Kant's monumental work. The word *Glaube* can mean both "belief" and "faith," but is better rendered here as the latter, because Kant was talking about a disposition to knowledge that could no longer rely on "science," which is an alternate translation of the German *Wissen*. A looser, but still accurate translation of this famous sentence might be "to abolish science to make room for faith." The original German sentence is as follows: "Ich musste also das Wissen, aufheben, um zum Glauben Platz zu bekommen."

[7]Kenneth A. Matthews, *Genesis 1-11:26*, New American Commentary (Nashville: Broadman & Holman, 1996), p. 237.

afterworld, so much as death as the "existential" limits of all our moral as well as cognitive possibilities. In other words, the post-Kantian philosophy of limits offers us a theoretical "wisdom" concerning what we cannot know. In eating the forbidden fruit, Adam and Eve bought into the lie of the serpent that they would be "as gods," that is, having infinite knowledge. Yet what they acquired instead was a finite self-consciousness that includes an awareness of death as the absolute and unsurpassable frontier of knowledge as a whole. It is a negative wisdom, one that the ancient Greeks understood as a tragic wisdom. Christian "knowledge," which does indeed transcend this tragic wisdom in the end because of our hope of the resurrection, can only be gained through faith in what God has shown and revealed in the miraculous events surrounding the death and raising up of Jesus.

Boyd, however, wants to rely on the created order itself to emphasize a continuity between what was known in the Garden and what we are capable of knowing now.

> It is a mistake to assume that reason is ever "unaided" by divine grace since it was created by divine grace and—although damaged by sin— never fully loses its efficacy. Our nature is more stable than the harmful effects of sin. As a result, all people can know basic truths about the world, God and morality. Regardless of religion, all people can reason correctly about the various operations of the natural world and the basic elements of morality as found in the natural law. (pp. 158-59)

This concluding statement by Boyd has the familiar ring of what during the eighteenth century was known as "natural theology." However, the knowledge gained through such a natural theology— usually confined to the fact of the existence of God and certain basic moral truths, a position often associated with the kind of knowledge Paul says in the opening section of Romans we have "no excuse" when it comes to disregarding it—is itself a limited knowledge. If after the fall grace itself would "naturally" operate in order to sustain us in such natural knowledge, the inherent problem of the fatal misuse of such knowledge for such ungodly or "unnatural" purposes (as Paul puts it) would not be the problem that it is.

Boyd recognizes the continuity between what might be called our "Edenic" understanding of things and the limited knowledge we can have today, but he gives far less credence to the corrosive and destructive capacities of natural reason itself, especially when it seeks a certain "wisdom" that only God possesses. Scripture is fairly clear on this matter.

Faith Seeking Understanding Response

Alan G. Padgett

I APPRECIATE MUCH OF BOYD'S CHAPTER and position, but that will not mean I have nothing to say in reply! I step very cautiously when people start talking about a "synthesis" of theology and philosophy, while at the same time I acknowledge that faith as basic trust and human reason as our ability to think things through always work together. Both are part of human nature.

Boyd argues that faith and reason should combine in a synthesis. That he writes in the long and varied tradition of Thomism is clear at many points, including his discussion of nature and grace, or reason and faith (and indeed the parallel he sees between these pairs).[1] In my response I will briefly address some of the main points where we agree and then summarize what I take to be Boyd's viewpoint. As is normal for such responses, I will manage to find something critical to say as well.

To begin with where we agree: that faith and reason can and should work together. We agree that reason needs faith in God and the work of the Holy Spirit to be "healed by grace" and restored to human reason's "original integrity" (p. 159). We both agree with Aquinas, and really all of classic Christian thinking, that our human species is "corrupted by sin" (pp. 144, 145, 158) in some way, and that this corruption does not exclude our reasoning. Finally, we agree that general revelation and common grace, both given to all by God primarily through the process of creation past and present, can lead some people to understand some truths about God and morality by a process of reasoning from what they know and observe. I would emphasize that these gifts of creational grace alone are not enough to provide us with saving faith and a sure knowledge of the promises of God. For saving faith and intimate knowledge of God one needs special acts of revelation and grace. Beyond general revelation,

---

[1] Readers who wish to begin to look into the life and thought of Aquinas may wish to see Fergus Kerr, *Thomas Aquinas: A Very Short Introduction* (Oxford: Oxford University Press, 2009).

God has provided special revelation to Israel and the church, for example in Jesus, in the inspired Scriptures, or in a word spoken or a prompting given to us within by the Holy Spirit. So far, so good.

While I was not clear what Boyd was trying to argue in every part of his chapter, my understanding of his basic viewpoint is this:

1. While human reasoning is corrupted by sin, it is not "radically corrupted by sin" (p. 144). For example, not all our thoughts or arguments are sinful. Further, reason does play some role in the reception and understanding of revelation, and thus through a process, and in part the mind does participate in our justification by faith before God.

2. Unaided by special acts of grace, humans are endowed by their Creator with enough reasoning capacity to work out some basic truths about God and the moral good. "All people know basic truths about morality" (p. 154).

3. "Grace perfects nature" so that the work of saving faith and God's special acts of grace are needed to make reason improve and grow to the extent that an intimate knowledge of God, and a more thorough knowledge of divine truth, become possible. Reason participates in our spiritual growth and discipleship.

4. What is more, "unaided reason" (p. 149), that is, unaided by *special* acts of divine grace, can understand the message of the gospel, and other communication and revelation from God, so that saving faith is possible in the first place.

5. Any person who properly reasons to a conclusion is participating in God's good creation as they are supposed to, and thus *is* aided by God's grace in creation, what we might call common grace or creational grace.[2]

6. Thus in coming to know more about God and live a godly life, a synthesis of reason and Christian faith takes place.

As presented here, these basic points seem reasonable, do they not? What problems could there be? Still, I have a few to bring up in this response.

Boyd does not do a very thorough job of explaining what his view means for the relationship between Christian theology and philosophy. It is at this level that I suspect there may be a problem, for the traditional

---

[2]See Aquinas, *Summa Theologiae* 1-2.109.1 (on the need for grace); a question also quoted by Boyd.

Thomistic view is that philosophy provides *a needed preamble* to Christian theology (or what Aquinas called *sacra doctrina*, holy teachings). Speaking only in terms of reason rather than philosophy per se, Boyd seems to agree with this common Thomistic view in his claim that reason is essential to understanding special revelation and to developing the knowledge of God.

My own view, in opposition to the standard Thomistic one, is that Christian theology and philosophy (or indeed any of the arts and sciences) are all *colleagues*. None of them sets the stage for the other, none is a necessary preamble or foundation for the others; while at the same time elements from one academic discipline may be necessary to the development and proper functioning of another. Computer science, for example, is very important to contemporary developments in economics or meteorology. Knowledge of chemistry is essential to the work of biologists, and physics is essential to chemistry. In the same way, no philosophy can be complete without considering the issue of religion. Conversely, Christian theology has consistently borrowed from, criticized and engaged various philosophies on a piecemeal, as-needed basis. I am happy to accept this much-needed *interdisciplinary* work, as long as the integrity and autonomy of each discipline is respected by the others. But I reject the idea that philosophy provides a *necessary foundation* for academic Christian theology. This is because no one philosophy can be trusted to do so, and *no source of knowledge other than Jesus Christ and the Holy Spirit working in special revelation is truly foundational for Christian theology.* This is why the Bible, as the inspired Word of God written by human beings, is so central to theology. Philosophy, while important, is not primary.

There is a similar point I would make concerning Boyd's discussion of the usefulness of unaided reason for Christian faith and thought. It is true that some people, in some cases, come to a point through using their reasoning powers where saving faith in Christ is the next step. Reason in these cases (and C. S. Lewis is a well-known example) does set the stage for the act of saving faith.[3] But why should I think that such

---

[3]See especially C. S. Lewis, *Surprised by Joy* (New York: Harcourt, 1956).

reasoning is *unaided* by God the Holy Spirit? Why should I think that reasoning is so separate from special acts of grace? After all, as a Wesleyan theologian I affirm the idea of "prevenient grace." This mode of grace involves special acts by the Holy Spirit, who draws each and every one of us often in ways unknown and always unique to each person. This gives everyone some opportunity to respond to God.[4] The fruit of prevenient grace, for many, is saving faith and justification, believing the gospel and being forgiven. Since I embrace this doctrine of prevenient grace, taught by many Christians over the centuries, I find it hard to believe that people like Lewis were using "unaided" reasoning powers. Sure, the capacity to reason is part of our common human nature. But why affirm that such reasoning is unaided by God's special acts of grace? We agree that good human reasoning does participate in common grace. Why stop there?

This raises a second problem. Boyd *seems* to imply that the relationship between Christian faith and reason maps one-to-one onto the relationship between philosophy and theology. In other words, I believe it is Boyd's view that the relationship between theology and philosophy mirrors the relationship between faith and reason. Yet it seems fairly obvious that these pairs have different relationships (reason and faith; philosophy and theology). To start with, reason is not the same thing as philosophy, since reason is used all over the place, including but not limited to every academic discipline. Faith is also not the same thing as theology. Even more importantly, theology, like philosophy and all the arts and sciences, draws upon *both* basic trust *and* human reason. Even if faith means "saving faith," Christian theology and Christian philosophy (of which Thomism is an important type) draw upon both faith *and* reason.

What is clear in his chapter is that, for Boyd, the relationship between nature and grace mirrors the relationship between faith and reason. Here I have another fundamental problem with his viewpoint. I believe that faith, understood as a basic capacity to trust, is a part of

---

[4]For a readable, brief introduction to the thought of John Wesley (including prevenient grace), see Steve Harper, *The Way to Heaven: The Gospel According to John Wesley* (Grand Rapids: Zondervan, 2003), previously published as *John Wesley's Message for Today*.

our human nature (I argue as much in my chapter). Boyd's analysis of "faith" is primarily in terms of Christian faith. I find that saving faith is a special application—no doubt healed by grace!—of a general human capacity for basic trust. The *capacity* for saving faith, as well as for loving and knowing God in an intimate way, is a part of our human nature. It is part of the common grace we all receive simply as human beings made in God's image.[5] In his discussion of three ways of using the word *faith* Boyd might perhaps agree with my point, but I am not sure (pp. 149-50). In any case, while nature and grace are *different*, they are never *separate*.[6]

But if the capacity for the act of faith and the habit of faith are part of our common human nature, how can the nature-grace dynamic·parallel the reason-faith dynamic? There seems to be a perplexing conflict at this point in Boyd's presentation.

To summarize some of my objections, then, I agree that reasoning as a kind of tool for understanding the word of promise from God has a role in the process of salvation and the ongoing life of faith. What I object to is that this be thought of as "unaided" reason. Further, I object to the idea that philosophy sets the stage for, or is a necessary foundation of, Christian theology. I do accept philosophy as an important *colleague* for theology, but likewise insist upon proper boundaries between them. Interdisciplinary work requires a proper independence with an expertise within a specific discipline, while at the same time being open to learning from and engaging with a different one. The danger of a "synthesis" between theology and philosophy is that philosophy will dominate the conversation, ask all the key questions, or provide the supposedly rational or scientific basis for theology's answers, as it did so often in the past within modern theology (e.g., Hegel, Christian personalism or Charles Hartshorne's process theology).[7] As much as Thomas admired

---

[5]See also Aquinas on this point, *Summa Theologiae* 1.93.4. He is overly narrow in arguing that human reason is the image of God in us; I think it is more than just that.

[6]My reading of Aquinas on this point is influenced by French theologian Henri de Lubac. De Lubac's own works are for specialists, but a brief introduction to his theology is found in David Grumett, *De Lubac: A Guide for the Perplexed* (London: T & T Clark, 2007).

[7]For my response to process theology on this particular point, see my chapter "Putting Reason in Its Place," in *Thy Nature and Thy Name is Love: Wesleyan and Process Theologies in Dialogue*, ed. Bryan Stone and Thomas Oord (Nashville: Abingdon, 2001), pp. 263-78.

and learned from philosophy, he did *not* make this mistake in his great *Summa Theologiae*.[8]

To conclude this response, I will point out again that Boyd and I are close in our views and agree on many central points. We both think that reason and faith, along with philosophy and theology, should work together. We accept the notion that philosophy and theology should be colleagues, but without one of them colonizing or dominating the other. However, we see the details of this relationship rather differently. For my part, I hold that faith *and* reason work together all the time, and do not mirror the relationship between creation and redemption (or if you like, nature and grace). No part of humanity is separate from the work of God's prevenient grace, and all creation is open to God's redemptive grace.

---

[8]Aquinas used the Aristotelian philosophy and science of his day but did not always follow these various arguments, being both positive and negative in his interaction with them. In the *Summa Theologiae* his primary goal was spiritual, theological and Christian, not philosophical.

Conclusion

A Brief Note on Disagreeing Christianly

Steve Wilkens

A FRIEND TELLS THE STORY of two groups of Christians who were embroiled in a theological dispute. The disagreement had become so rancorous that a denominational official had to step in and call the warring sides into a meeting. On the day of the meeting the two groups seated themselves on opposite sides of the table, ready for battle. The body language signaled the strong likelihood that the discussion would end exactly where it had started—in a bitter standoff.

The moderator opened the conversation by asking each participant to describe how they saw their ministry as their response to God's grace. On the surface, this request appeared to have little to do with the issue at hand. In reality, it had a great deal of relevance, because by the time the discussion transitioned to the theological conflict, the participants had reframed their disagreements. They no longer saw the people on the other side of the table as opponents but as family. I don't want to sugar-coat the result. Their doctrinal differences still remained at the end of the talks. However, because of the moderator's wise leadership, disagreement did not result in schism. Instead, they were able to recognize that those with whom they disagreed had come to their conclusions from a shared interest in discerning God's truth and a common motive of building up the body of Christ.

I keep this story in the back of my mind because a large part of my work involves discussions of "hot-button" issues, ideas that are vital to our understanding of God, ourselves and creation. This book is just one example of such forays into perennial issues of contention. Obviously, I find a great deal of value in these sorts of discussions, and I pray that this book has provided the opportunity to listen in on a sustained conversation between thoughtful Christians. However, as we have seen, those thoughtful Christians disagree on matters pertaining to grace, revelation, reason, salvation and a number of other important doctrinal loci that cut close to spiritually sensitive areas.

Recognizing the areas where thoughtful Christians have disagreed across the centuries is useful for tracing the genealogical lines within our family of faith. It is also vital to our own process of coming to a more informed understanding of our own faith commitments. However, if we focus only on the disagreements we may unintentionally imply that the expected response is either cynicism or division. Neither is desirable for Christians, although both are all too common. Therefore, we want to foreground some elements that allow us to put the disagreements within this book into a context that will allow us to reap the benefits of such discussions.

First, while doctrinal divergences can lead to divisiveness or despair about discerning the truth, Christianity is more than doctrine. It is also about the way we live and act. It is also about the virtues that characterize the Christian life and the actions that should result from them. Christians tend to have greater unity and clarity about these matters, and thus attention to Christian character and practices can function as a healthy counterweight to factionalism and cynicism. To highlight just one example, implicit throughout this discussion is a call to humility. All three authors make the point that God's revelation should not be confused with our theology. While revelation is a trustworthy authority, our theology is subject to error. Thus, while each of these authors advocates a different view of how philosophy relates to theology, they also acknowledge the need for humility in our intellectual endeavors. Human fallibility requires that our theological positions, even as we offer a vigorous defense of them, should always be open to revision. As a result, a sense of humility is tacitly present in the structure of this book, in which each author subjects his views to the close scrutiny of the other two rather than simply preaching to a choir of supporters. In short, advocacy of what we believe to be true should be conditioned by a spirit of humility, fairness, openness and courage. Such qualities function as a hedge against division.

A second thing often overlooked in cases in which we juxtapose divergent viewpoints is that, despite the obvious differences, these positions also occupy vast tracts of mutual agreement. Indeed, the debate within the covers of this book would not be possible unless the contributors converged on so many fundamental theological ideas. One important agreement is their rejection of the modernist optimism about unaided reason. The Enlightenment believed that reason, once liberated from reliance on external authorities such as Scripture and tradition, would successfully lead us to truth. In contrast, all three perspectives in this book reject that degree of autonomy for reason. Thus, even if our authors disagree, for example, about whether philosophical arguments are of evangelistic value, none claims that intellectual assent to a set of ideas, no matter how consistent with Christian doctrine, suffices for salvation. To know God as logical principle or abstract power falls short of a robust and saving knowledge of God.

A second vital area of agreement is that, although all of this book's authors reject the authority of autonomous reason, each acknowledges that our intellectual capacities are a gift from God that comes with a demand for responsible stewardship. In fact, their reflective chapters exemplify the conviction that Christian faith is not incidental to a motivation to know but is intrinsic to it. Thus, in presenting their case for how we should think about the relationship between philosophy and faith, none of the authors dismisses scholarship. To the contrary, they call upon intellectual giants of the past and present, both theologians and philosophers, to bolster their arguments. Moreover, the scholarship of Christian thinkers cited from across the historical spectrum is an indicator that our authors are not idiosyncratic in their affirmation of the intellect. The footnotes witness to the reality that each of this book's three positions has a view of the intellect sufficiently vigorous to produce great philosophers and theologians. In other words, no matter where you look on the spectrum of beliefs about the relationship of faith and philosophy, you find Christians, including our three authors, who see scholarly engagement of intellectual issues as a legitimate expression of Christian commitment.

A third area of agreement for all three positions is that faith has epistemic value. There is consensus that we do not know as fully apart from faith as when we are embraced by it. This is related to the fact that each author acknowledges that knowledge is never fully independent of volition, and that until our will undergoes redemption, true understanding will face impediments that cannot be removed except by faith. Related to this, we find concord among the three views in the belief that, regardless of the degree that intellect can (or cannot) nudge us toward salvation, the latter is always dependent on grace. This helps account for the rejection of Enlightenment confidence. No matter how much we can untangle ourselves from biases—whether cultural, historical or otherwise—we cannot escape the selfish and rebellious biases imposed by our own distorted will in order to know clearly. Thus Christians may disagree about when grace comes into play in our movement toward salvation or whether our will is capable of cooperating with God's in this process, but the utter necessity of grace is not contested.

A corollary to the last point is that all three positions affirm that we cannot speak clearly and completely about either faith or philosophy apart from knowledge of ourselves as finite and sinful. This critical self-knowledge conditions all discussions about the place of reason by warning us that every individual and age is subject to the pretension that it has overcome the arrested intellectual development of the past and has finally "got it." In other words, we find agreement among our contributors that forgetfulness about our state of sinfulness and finitude leads to fruitless attempts to establish ourselves as gods. The flipside of this idolatry points to one final area of unity in our three views. The ultimate point of knowledge is not self-aggrandizement but the worship and glorification of God.

Like the story at the beginning of this chapter, this book involves disagreement. In both cases, theological differences remain at the end. However, those in our opening story only later recognized something that, we hope, has been a clear but consistent undercurrent throughout this book. While the contributors may dissent on the conclusions of other views, they do so without questioning motives. They have listened and responded carefully to one another instead of isolating themselves from alternative voices. And even though their assignment for this text specified that they give special attention to areas where they, and Christians across the historical timeline, have found reasons to draw differing conclusions, it should be evident that this was a family discussion. The centrality of faith, the need for and provision of God's grace for understanding and salvation, the recognition of human fallibility and fallenness, and the recognition that the human intellect's activities honor God when functioning within the intended boundaries are just a few areas of unity. Trust in these truths keeps other uncertainties from degenerating into cynicism. Humility and the recognition of the shared foundation on which we build keep differences from dividing us.

List of Contributors

Craig A. Boyd (PhD, St. Louis University) is chair of core curriculum and general studies at St. Louis University. He has published two books: *A Shared Morality: A Narrative Defense of Natural Law Ethics* (Brazos Press, 2007) and *Visions of Agapé: Problems and Possibilities in Divine and Human Love* (Ashgate, 2008). His journal articles have appeared in *American Catholic Philosophical Quarterly, The Modern Schoolman, New Blackfriars, Studies in Science and Theology, Theology and Science* and *Zygon: Journal of Religion and Science*. His research interests include medieval philosophy, natural law, virtue ethics, evolution, and issues in science and theology.

Alan G. Padgett (DPhil, Oxford University) is professor of systematic theology at Luther Seminary in St. Paul, Minnesota, and a minister in the United Methodist Church. His research and writing often explore the relationships between Scripture, Christian theology, philosophy and the sciences. He has authored, coauthored or edited eleven books and more than one hundred scholarly articles and essays, most recently the *Blackwell Companion to Science and Christianity* (coedited with James Stump).

Carl A. Raschke (PhD, Harvard University) is professor of religious studies at the University of Denver. He is the author of numerous books and hundreds of articles on topics ranging from postmodernism to popular religion and culture to technology and society. He is the author of *Fire and Roses: Postmodernity and the Thought of the Body* (State University of New York Press, 1995), *The Engendering God: Male and Female Faces of God* (Westminster John Knox, 1995), *The Digital Revolution and the Coming of the Postmodern University* (Routledge, 2002) and *The Next Reformation: Why Evangelicals Must Embrace Postmodernity* (Baker Academic, 2004). He is cofounder and senior editor of *The Journal for Cultural and Religious Theory* and has been involved recently in the development of national online learning initiatives, including the Syllabus Institute.

Index

Finding the Textbook You Need

The IVP Academic Textbook Selector
is an online tool for instantly finding the IVP books
suitable for over 250 courses across 24 disciplines.

www.ivpress.com/academic/textbookselector